KB087887

Letters
from
Korean
History

Notes on the English translation

Korean personal names, place names, proper nouns and common nouns have been transliterated according to the Revised Romanization of Korean system, introduced by the South Korean government in 2000. The only exceptions are names that are widely recognized in other forms, such as Syngman Rhee (Lee Seungman) or Kim Ilsung (Kim Ilseong). Two of the most common Korean surnames, Kim and Park, have been left in their conventional forms, rather than Gim and Bak (which would be their spellings according to the Revised Romanization system). The surname Lee, meanwhile, is transliterated as Yi before 1945, in accordance with convention (for example, Yi Seonggye), and then in the more modern form of Lee after 1945, taking Korean liberation as a somewhat arbitrary dividing line. Surnames are listed before first names, in the Korean style, with the singular, Americanized exception of Syngman Rhee.

The ages of individuals are listed in accordance with the original Korean text of *Letters from Korean History*, which naturally follows the Korean convention for age calculation. This means that figures given are generally one year higher than what would be considered the corresponding "Western" age.

Letters
from
Korean
History

③

Joseon - From founding to later years

Park Eunbong

CUM LIBRO 책과함께

History in Northeast Asia is like a minefield. Riddled with unresolved issues, controversies, disputed territory and conflicting ideologies, it often breeds acrimony among governments and peoples in the region. Within many countries, too, blind nationalism, political bias and censorship constantly threaten to distort the picture painted by historians of their country's past and, by extension, present. Creating a balanced narrative in the midst of such tension and conflicting perspectives is no easy task. But that is what Park Eunbong appears to have done in *Letters from Korean History*.

Offering children and young readers an unbiased version of their past is one of the kindest and most responsible ways of helping them grow into broad-minded citizens, capable of sustaining peace and cooperation in a region - and world - that grows more interconnected every year but still bears unhealed historical scars and bruises. In Korea, such a history also offers context that can put the country's current state of division - only sixty-seven years old as of 2015 - into wider perspective.

Making any Korean book accessible to readers of English through translation is a privilege. The same goes for *Letters from Korean History*. In a series of letters addressed to a young reader overseas, the author adopts a conversational style of writing that conveys the ups and downs, ins and outs of Korean history with ease. But while the language is highly accessible, the content is never rendered simplistic or patronizing, and issues that lose some other historians in a fog of

nationalism are navigated by Park with the kind of healthy detachment and clarity that inspires confidence in the reader.

Progressing from the stones and bones of prehistory all the way to the turbulent twentieth century in the course of five volumes, *Letters from Korean History* can be browsed as a reference text or plowed through from beginning to end. As with most histories that cover such a long period, the density of information increases as the narrative approaches the present. The relatively recent Joseon period, for example, accounts for two of the five volumes (III and IV), rich as it is in events and meticulously recorded historical data.

Letters from Korean History has been a great success in its native country among Korean readers. I hope that this translation will now be of help to ethnic Koreans overseas, others interested in Korea or history in general, Koreans looking to study history and English at the same time, and anybody else who believes that exploring the past is a good way to try and make sense of the confusing, flawed and wonderful present.

Ben Jackson
May, 2016

To readers of 'Letters from Korean History'

Letters from Korean History is a series of some seventy letters covering a period that stretches from prehistory to the present. Unlike most introductions to Korean history, it takes a theme-based approach: each theme functions as a window onto a particular period. The use of several different windows offering various perspectives onto the same period is meant to help the reader form her or his own more complete picture of that part of history. For example, "Buddhism, key to the culture of the Three Kingdoms" and "Silla, land of the bone-rank system," two letters in Volume I, offer two different ways of understanding Silla history: a religious perspective via Buddhism; and a social caste-based perspective by way of the bone-rank system. My hope is that, after reading both letters and exploring these two separate approaches, readers will come closer to gaining a comprehensive understanding of Silla. The more diverse the windows opened, the more helpful this should be in the forming of a complete image.

Letters from Korean History places equal emphasis on aspects such as culture, everyday life, society and social segments with habitually low historical profiles, such as women and children. This is an important difference to conventional introductory histories, which naturally tend towards narratives centered on ruling classes by prioritizing political history.

I have also attempted to portray Korean history not as that of a single nation in isolation but as part of world history as a whole, and to adopt a perspective that places humans as just one species in the universe and nature. This is why the first letter begins not with prehistory on the Korean Peninsula but with the birth of the human race on Earth. The connection with world history is maintained throughout the five volumes, in which Korea's interactions, relationships and

points of comparison with the rest of the world are constantly explored.

The single most distinct aspect of *Letters from Korean History* is that, unlike most general histories, which make passing references to characters and dates, it depicts Korea's past through a series of engaging stories. It is my hope that these will help readers feel like direct witnesses to historical scenes as they unfold. All content is based on historical materials, either in their original form or adapted without distortion. Sources include key texts such as *Samguk sagi* ("History of the Three Kingdoms"), *Samguk yusa* ("Memorabilia of the Three Kingdoms"), *Goryeosa* ("History of Goryeo") and *Joseon wangjo sillok* ("Royal Annals of the Joseon Dynasty"), as well as a variety of literary anthologies, letters, journals and epigraphs.

The English version of *Letters from Korean History* is published for young readers overseas who are curious about Korea and its people, and for young Korean readers keen to learn more about their own history while improving their language skills as global citizens. I hope that readers will not feel obliged to start at the beginning of Volume I and plow all the way through; rather, each letter contains a historical episode in its own right, and can be chosen and read according to the reader's particular area of interest. The text is complemented by plenty of photos and illustrations, giving a more vivid sense of history - reading the captions that accompany these should enhance the sense of historical exploration.

I very much hope that this book will become a useful source of guidance for young readers, wherever they may be.

Park Eunbong

May, 2016

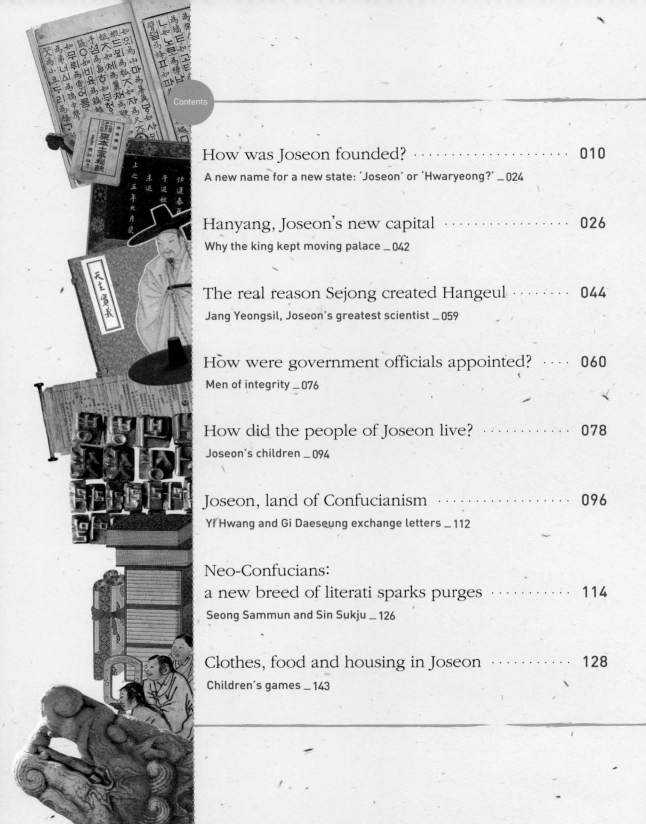

Contents

CHAPTER 1

How was Joseon founded?

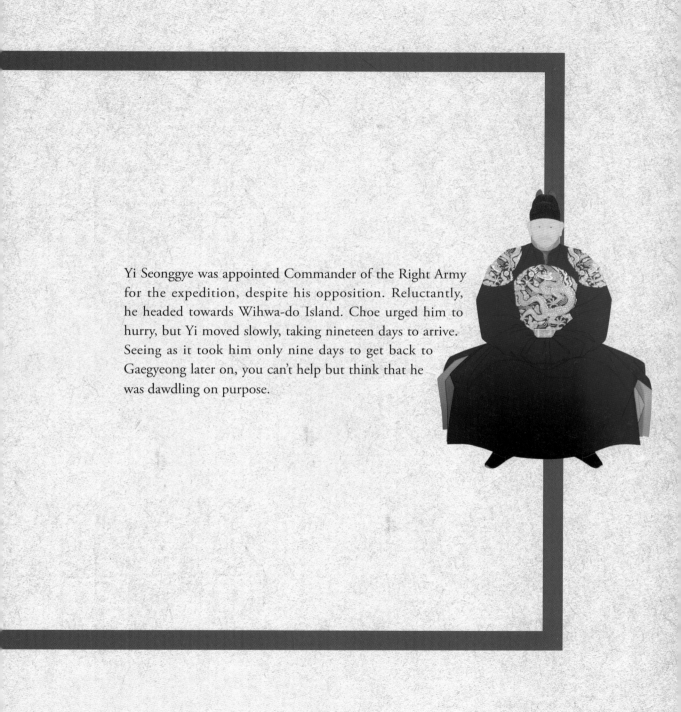

Yi Seonggye was appointed Commander of the Right Army for the expedition, despite his opposition. Reluctantly, he headed towards Wihwa-do Island. Choe urged him to hurry, but Yi moved slowly, taking nineteen days to arrive. Seeing as it took him only nine days to get back to Gaegyeong later on, you can't help but think that he was dawdling on purpose.

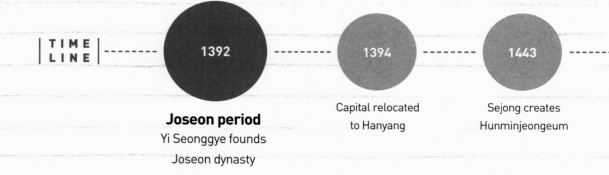

TIME
LINE

1392

Joseon period
Yi Seonggye founds
Joseon dynasty

1394

Capital relocated
to Hanyang

1443

Sejong creates
Hunminjeongeum

Joseon was the successor of Goryeo. It differed from its predecessor in several ways, however, starting with its founding. The establishment of these two states makes an interesting comparison. You will remember how Goryeo was founded: at the end of the Later Three Kingdoms period, when Hugoguryeo, Hubaekje and Silla had been fighting for around forty-five years, Wanggeon united them all through a series of wars and founded Goryeo.

While Goryeo came into being through war and the unification of the Later Three Kingdoms, Joseon emerged in different circumstances: a change of ruling class in one country. All this began with an incident known as the "withdrawal from Wihwa-do Island." Its protagonist was Yi Seonggye, who later became the first king of Joseon. Let's start by taking a look at the withdrawal, which proved to be the first step on the path to establishing the new state.

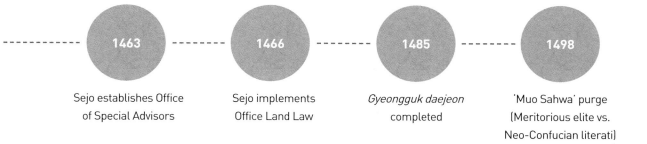

1463 Sejo establishes Office of Special Advisors

1466 Sejo implements Office Land Law

1485 *Gyeongguk daejeon* completed

1498 'Muo Sahwa' purge (Meritorious elite vs. Neo-Confucian literati)

Goryeo at this time was unsettled. It had begun an attack on Liaodong in April 1388 according to the lunar calendar. Liaodong lies beyond the Amnokgang River, on the way into China, and has long been of great military importance to both countries.

Eventually, 70,000 Goryeo troops set off for Liaodong. The Goryeo military was headed by three men: Choe Yeong was supreme commander of the Armies of the Eight Provinces, with Jo Minsu and Yi Seonggye as his deputies. King U of Goryeo went with them. The king and Choe stopped and stayed in Pyeongyang, on the way, while Yi and Jo led their forces all the way to the Amnokgang, at the center of which lies Wihwa-do. Here, the Goryeo army struck camp.

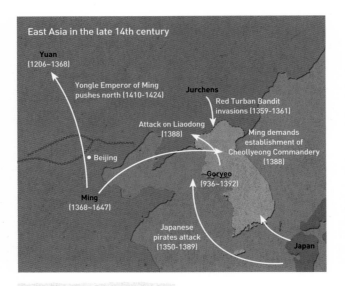

East Asia in the late 14th century

Yuan
(1206~1368)

Yongle Emperor of Ming
pushes north (1410-1424)

Jurchens

Red Turban Bandit
invasions (1359-1361)

Attack on Liaodong
(1388)

Ming demands
establishment of
Cheollyeong Commandery
(1388)

• Beijing

Goryeo
(936~1392)

Ming
(1368~1647)

Japanese
pirates attack
(1350-1389)

Japan

Withdrawal from Wihwa-do: first step toward the founding of Joseon

Why would Goryeo have set out to attack Liadong? The answer lies in its relationship with China at the time, when much of the latter was ruled by the Ming Empire. Ming was driving the Yuan Empire north and gaining control of an increasingly large part of today's China. It took a dim view of Goryeo and was watching it with suspicion lest it join forces with Yuan in the north and threaten the new order. Ming made persistently difficult demands of Goryeo, demanding horses, gold and silver for use in the fight against Yuan.

One day, Ming unilaterally laid claim to the area north of Cheollyeong, the part of Gangwon-do Province that now lies in North Korea and is known as Anbyeon, and declared that it would administer the region from then on. This area had once been controlled by the Yuan Commandery Headquarters at Ssangseong, at a time when Goryeo had been its vassal state and Yuan was meddling in every last detail of Goryeo politics.

As you know, King Gongmin, whose policy was to oppose Yuan and gain autonomy, had won back this territory by

Yuan Commandery Headquarters at Ssangseong

Yuan built this outpost at Ssangseong, in the Hwaju area (today's Yeongheung in Hamgyeong-do Province), at a time when Goryeo was its vassal state. The area was inhabited by Goryeo people and Jurchens, living together. In 1356, King Gongmin successfully attacked the commandery and won back the region. At this moment, Yi Seonggye's father, Yi Jachun, who had been working as an official at the commandery, distinguished himself by helping Gongmin and contributing greatly to the Goryeo victory. In recognition of his service, Yi was awarded the title "military commander of the northeast region." From then on, his family grew gradually more powerful.

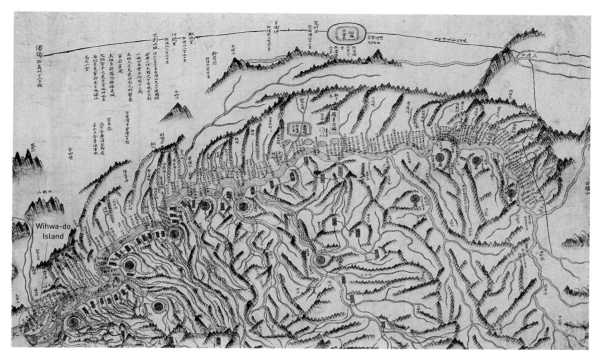

Wihwa-do
Island

Wihwa-do Island as
marked on 'Amnokgang
gyedo'
This Joseon-era map
depicts the Amnokgang
region. Try to find Wihwa-
do: it's the small island
marked by a red circle.
Those crossing the river
from Wihwa-do into China
arrive in Liaodong.
– National Museum of Korea

fighting off Yuan forces. Now, Ming was claiming the land again on the grounds that it had once belonged to Yuan. Ming told Goryeo it would set up a government office, known as the Cheollyeong Commandery, to manage the area north of Cheollyeong.

This made the Goryeo royal court even more worried about a potential Ming invasion. The first thing it did was send an envoy, Park Uijung, to try and change Ming's mind. After Park had set off for China, however, the Goryeo court became divided into two camps of opinion.

"There's no way we can give away the land north of Cheollyeong," some ministers claimed. "We can no longer meet Ming's exorbitant demands, so we need to preempt it by attacking Liaodong."

"Ming is a huge empire," others countered. "We mustn't try and fight it."

The attack on Liaodong was advocated by King U and Choe Yeong but opposed by Yi Seonggye, who gave four reasons why it was impossible:

"Firstly, small countries should not take on larger opponents. Secondly, you can't call up reserve military forces in summer because the peasants are too busy farming. Thirdly, using our entire army to attack Liaodong will leave other areas vulnerable to attack by Japanese pirates. Fourthly, the monsoon rain will melt the glue on our arrows and increase the risk of disease spreading among our forces."

Yi's reasons have become known as the "Four Impossibles." But King U and Choe Yeong ignored them. When the king and the highest-ranking official in the land called for an attack on Liaodong it was bound to go ahead, no matter how many opposed it. Ultimately, Goryeo began its attack before its envoy, Park Uijung, had even returned from Ming.

Yi Seonggye was appointed commander of the exhibition, despite his opposition. Reluctantly, he headed towards Wihwa-do Island. Choe urged him to hurry, but Yi moved slowly, taking nineteen days to arrive. Seeing as it took him only nine days to get back to Gaegyeong later on, you can't help but think that he was dawdling on purpose.

Even once he had reached Wihwa-do, Yi had no intention of crossing the Amnokgang and invading Liaodong. Instead, he struck camp and spent fourteen days just surveying his surroundings. In the meantime, he sent one of his men to U and Choe in Pyeongyang and asked them to reconsider.

"Many of my troops are starving to death and the water is deep, making it difficult to march," he said. "Please give us permission to withdraw immediately."

But the answer was very brief: they told Yi to get on with it. It was then that Yi finally made up his mind. He gathered his troops and spoke to them.

The withdrawal from Wihwa-do
Yi Seonggye and his men ride back toward Gaegyeong after turning their horses around. This was an act of treason against Goryeo and the first step toward founding a new state.

"If we invade Ming territory, this will bring immediate disaster to the country and the people. I asked for permission to withdraw, but the king ignored me and Choe Yeong is old, so his mind is clouded and he won't listen. So don't you think we ought to get rid of the villains surrounding the king and bring peace to the country?"

Yi's subordinates were unanimous in their answer:

"The fate of the country depends on you alone, general. We will do as you order."

Finally, Yi turned his horse back from Wihwa-do. His destination was now no longer Liaodong, across the river, but Gaegyeong, the capital. He had become a traitor.

This incident is known as the "withdrawal from Wihwa-do." Yi Seonggye had hoisted a banner of treason and taken the first step toward founding a new state.

Meanwhile, King U and Choe Yeong in Pyeongyang heard the news that Yi had turned his forces around. They hurried back to Gaegyeong. Choe gathered his remaining men and tried to stop Yi, but was overwhelmed. Yi captured the capital, sent Choe into exile in Gobong (today's Goyang) in Gyeonggi-do Province, and banished King U to Ganghwa-do Island.

A while later, Choe was brought to Gaegyeong and executed. Then a

Tomb of Choe Yeong
Choe was renowned as a brave general and an incorruptible official. He was also King U's father-in-law. Choe's tomb is located on Mt. Daejasan in Goyang, Gyeonggi-do Province.

seventy-three-years-old man, he met his death with such calm and dignity that those who witnessed it bowed their heads in respect. On the day he died, even the children cried. Passers-by who saw his corpse, abandoned by the side of the road, got off their horses to pay their respects.

Yi Seonggye's allies

Joseon was finally founded four years after the withdrawal from Wihwa-do. In the meantime, Goryeo was swept up in a whirlwind of change. At the eye of the storm stood Yi Seonggye, who remained there thanks to the steady support of various people. So who were they?

Firstly, the new leader was backed by several military figures, men who had become famous after distinguishing themselves in service against the Red Turban and Japanese invasions. Without their support, the withdrawal probably couldn't have succeeded.

Secondly, he was supported by men such as Jeong Dojeon, Jo Jun and Nam Eun, critics of Goryeo who dreamed of reform. These people are referred to collectively as the New Gentry (*Sinjin Saryu*).

The New Gentry shared their own set of unique characteristics: they had actively studied and embraced Neo-Confucianism; they had entered government by passing the

The New Gentry
This faction appeared during the reign of King Gongmin. As I mentioned, the king enlisted the help of a monk named Sin Don in order to help him escape Yuan's interference. He also appointed several fresh and talented young men, who became collectively known as the New Gentry (*Sinjin Saryu*). Other Korean names for them included the *Sinheung Sadaebu*, the *Sinjin Sadaebu* and the *Sinheung Yusin*.

state examination; they advocated keeping Yuan at a distance and allying with Ming; and they longed for domestic reform.

Yi Seonggye joined forces with the New Gentry and began pushing for reform. The latter were divided into two factions, moderates and radicals, when it came to the question of who should replace King U. The former was represented by Jeong Mongju and the latter by Jeong Dojeon and Jo Jun. King Chang, the nine-year-old son of U, eventually ascended the throne in accordance with the wishes of the moderate faction, but rivalry between the two sides only grew fiercer as time

 ## The Rank Land Law

The most serious social problem in the late Goryeo period was the monopolization of land by a minority of powerful and tyrannical families. Known as *gwonmun sejok*, these clans owned large tracts of of land known as *nongjang*.

After the withdrawal from Wihwa-do, Yi Seonggye and the New Gentry had to get rid of the *nongjang*: this was the only way they could gain wider support. They therefore abolished Goryeo's Field and Woodland Rank Law and replaced it with a new one: the Rank Land Law.

How did the old and new laws differ? They were both based on the principle of the state granting government officials the right to levy taxes on certain pieces of land in exchange for services rendered. But while the former applied to all the land in the country, the latter applied only to that in Gyeonggi-do, the province around the new capital. As a result, the state grew financially healthy by levying taxes directly from all other provinces. The rate of taxation was set at one tenth of what tenants produced on the land, greatly easing their burden.

went by.

Yi Seonggye removed Chang from the throne, claiming that he should not rule because he and his father were descended from Sin Don rather than King Gongmin, and replaced him with his own relative, King Gongyang. As you will probably have guessed, however, Gongyang was king only by name: real power lay with Yi and his supporters.

A new dynasty and the founding of Joseon

After placing Gongyang on the throne, Yi and the radical faction began calling for a dynastic revolution. This meant bringing down the Wang dynasty and replacing it with the Yi family, effectively destroying Goryeo and establishing a new state. The moderates, however, opposed overthrowing Goryeo, despite agreeing on the need for reform. In the end, the radicals killed Jeong Mongju, the leading figure in the moderate faction, as he crossed Seonjukgyo Bridge one night in Gaegyong.

Around three months after Jeong's death, Yi Seonggye became king. Goryeo, which had lasted some 500 years, faded into history and was replaced by a new state. This state belonged not only to Yi Seonggye but to Jeong Dojeon, Jo Jun and the other members of the New Gentry who had supported him.

King U and King Chang
Were kings U and Chang really descended from Sin Don? According to *Goryeosa*, they were. This claim, however, was fabricated in order to emphasize the legitimacy of the founding of Joseon. Nowhere is there any firm evidence to back it up.

The death of Jeong Mongju
This scene from the Joseon book *Oryun haengsildo* ("Five Moral Rules with Illustrations") depicts Jeong's death. *Oryun haengsildo* praises individuals who observed the Three Bonds and Five Relationships promoted by Confucianism. Despite his opposition to the founding of Joseon, Jeong was later held up as a loyal subject who had maintained his integrity, hence his appearance in *Oryun haengsildo*.

Seonjukgyo Bridge This stone bridge, which dates from the early Goryeo period, was originally called Seonjigyo. Yi Seonggye's son, Bangwon, had his men assassinate Jeong Mongju here after Yi failed to bring Jeong round to his side. Jeong was fifty-six at the time. One story tells that a stem of bamboo sprouted up by the bridge after his death; this is how it acquired the name Seonjukgyo, which means "bridge of the good bamboo."

Remember how I mentioned that Joseon was different from Goryeo, which was formed by unifying divided nations after a long war? Joseon was established through a successful military coup d'état. Because of this difference, opinion is divided even today over whether the withdrawal from Wihwa-do was the right thing to do, and whether the founding of Joseon was a natural turn of events.

Some say the withdrawal was nothing more than a coup d'état, that the founding of Joseon was merely a superficial change of monarch, and that society as a whole barely changed. Others are full of praise for the withdrawal, calling it the first step in a revolutionary process of creating a new society. Still others claim that the new state brought clear changes of a kind, albeit not dramatic development to society

as a whole. So who is right? You might want to think about this for yourself.

Oh — you may be wondering what happened to Park Uijung, the envoy dispatched to Ming. In the end, he came back with an answer: Ming had decided not to demand the establishment of Cheollyeong Commandery. Which means the attack on Liaodong had not even been necessary after all. And without the attack, there would have been no withdrawal from Wihwa-do and no founding of Joseon. Then again, maybe without the assault, Ming wouldn't have backed down so easily. Wasn't it the planned attack that gave the empire the message that Goryeo was not to be messed with and caused it to abandon the plan to set up Cheollyeong Commandery? History has a habit of biting its own tail like this, you know.

Gyeonggijeon Shrine and Taejo Yi Seonggye
History features several characters who used military force to threaten the established order. In the distant past, during the Goryeo period, we find Jeong Jungbu with his Military Officers' Rebellion. A more recent example is that of Park Chunghee, who became president by way of a military coup on May 16, 1960. Some of these men succeeded in grabbing power; others failed. Yi Seonggye is an example of the former. If his gamble had failed, he would have been executed. The photo on the left is of Gyeonggijeon Shrine, which contains Yi's portrait. The shrine stands in Jeonju, Jeollabuk-do Province. The progenitor of the Jeonju Yi clan is also enshrined here: Yi Seonggye's ancestors lived in Jeonju for generations, before moving north to Hamgyeong-do Province.

A new name for a new state: 'Joseon' or 'Hwaryeong?'

For quite some time, the new state kept the name Goryeo. When Taejo Yi Seonggye became king, at a ceremony on July 17, 1392 according to the lunar calendar at Suchanggung Palace in Gaegyeong, he made the following declaration:

"We will keep the name Goryeo and continue to follow its laws and systems."

Yi had decided to act cautiously, because a lot of people were less than happy with the dynastic change. Presently, however, he received a letter from Ming asking what the new state was called.

Unable to answer that they were using the name of the previous state, Yi and the New Gentry came up with two possible new names: Joseon and Hwaryeong. They wrote them both down and sent an envoy to Ming with the message that they would adopt whichever name their giant neighbor preferred. The former was derived from those of Dangun Joseon, Gija Joseon and Wiman Joseon, while the latter was the name of Yi Seonggye's birthplace, which is now named Yeongheung and located in Hamgyeong-do Province, North Korea. At the time, it was called Hwaryeong.

The following year, in 1393, the envoy returned from Ming with an answer.

"The name Joseon is beautiful and has a long history. If you use it and let your people prosper in accordance with the will of Heaven, your descendants will flourish for years to come."

That's how the new state was named Joseon. Does it seem absurd that Yi and his supporters asked another country to name their own?

Hamheung Bongung
This was the home of Yi Seonggye's father. The Joseon royal family held regular ancestral rites here. It is located in Hamheung, Hamgyeongnam-do Province.

No Korean state had ever asked China to name it, neither in the Three Kingdoms period nor the Goryeo period. So why would Yi Seonggye and the New Gentry have asked Ming to do this? Because they knew how sensitive relations with their neighbor were at the time, and were sending the message that their new state, unlike Goryeo, would not attack Liaodong but settle for the position of a submissive, smaller state, while asking for recognition in return.

CHAPTER 2

Hanyang,
Joseon's new capital

As soon as he returned to Gaegyeong, Yi issued an order for the relocation of his capital to Hanyang.

That's how, after various ups and downs, Hanyang was chosen as capital of the new state of Joseon. It was picked for the beautiful configuration of the surrounding mountains and rivers, its central position on the Korean Peninsula, and for the ease with which taxes levied in the provinces could be delivered by boat.

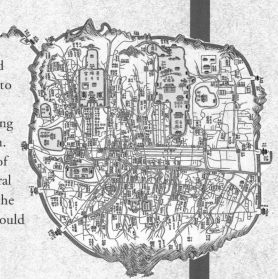

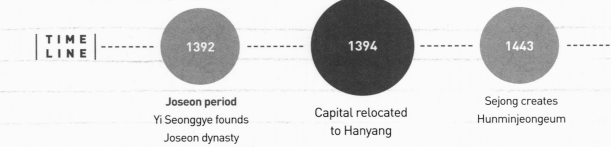

TIME
LINE

1392

Joseon period
Yi Seonggye founds
Joseon dynasty

1394

Capital relocated
to Hanyang

1443

Sejong creates
Hunminjeongeum

Have you ever heard people talk of the six hundredth anniversary of Seoul becoming the Korean capital? It's something we hear quite often in Korea today. But it's wrong. In fact, Seoul was a capital way back in the Three Kingdoms Period, long before the advent of Joseon. Hopefully you'll recall that Wiryeseong, the first capital of Baekje, was located in today's Seoul. In other words, Seoul was the capital of Baekje for some five hundred years, from the founding of the state until the relocation of the royal court to Gongju. In the Goryeo period it was named Namgyeong, meaning "southern capital," and served as the state's second capital. Which all means that we should be talking about the two-thousandth anniversary of Seoul as the nation's capital, not the six-hundredth.

In the Joseon period, Seoul was named Hanyang or Hanseong. Today, let's take a closer look at the Joseon capital and find out how it differed from today's metropolis.

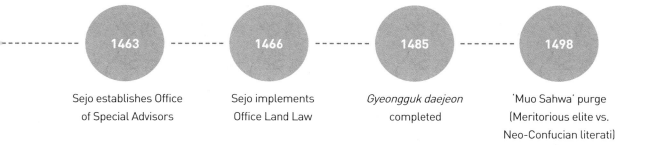

1463	1466	1485	1498
Sejo establishes Office of Special Advisors	Sejo implements Office Land Law	*Gyeongguk daejeon* completed	'Muo Sahwa' purge (Meritorious elite vs. Neo-Confucian literati)

When Joseon was first founded, it took the old Goryeo capital, Gaegyeong, as its own. A little while later, though, it suddenly relocated its royal court to Hanyang. Why? Because of a firm conviction on the part of Taejo Yi Seonggye that the capital had to be moved.

Yi must have wanted to escape Gaegyeong after the bloodbath he had created there. He had killed all of the Wang family, Goryeo's former rulers, and all those who remained loyal to them. Many people in Gaegyeong, moreover, harbored feelings of nostalgia for Goryeo. Yi needed to move somewhere else and make a new start. On top of this were various rumors claiming that Gaegyeong's luck had run out, or that there would be a coup if the capital weren't relocated - all of which

Dragon's head at Suchanggung Palace
This carved dragon's head once guarded the royal palace in Gaegyeong. It was here that Taejo Yi Seonggye acceded to the throne as Joseon's first king. With its body hidden and only its head revealed, the dragon seems poised and ready to soar up into the sky at any moment. Today, it is located in the front yard of the Koryo Museum in Gaeseong (the current name of Gaegyeong).

Ha Ryun
Ha was one of Taejo Yi Seonggye's most trusted lieutenants. He also won the favor of Yi's son, Bang-won, by playing a key role in helping him eliminate Jeong Dojeon and take the throne to become King Taejong. Ha studied Neo-Confucianism, but was also well-versed in *pungsujiri*.

'Gyeonggangbu imjindo' ('Donggugyeodo')
Produced in the nineteenth century, at the end of the Joseon period, this picture shows Hanyang and its surrounding area. Hanyang is marked by the Chinese characters "京城" ("Gyeongseong"), while Gangnam, which literally means "south of the river" and is now the most prosperous part of Seoul, was not yet part of the city.
– Kyujanggak Institute for Korean Studies

provided Yi with further motivation.

Conditions for a new capital

Yi ordered his lieutenants to choose a site for his new capital. The first candidate to emerge was Gyeryongsan, an area that corresponds to today's Sindoan in Chungcheongnam-do Province. But Ha Ryun, one of Yi's favorite lieutenants, strongly opposed it.

"Gyeryongsan is small and cramped. Its land is barren, it's hard to access and it's far from the Geumgang River. Life for the people will be tough there."

The next candidate was Muak, near Mt. Ansan in what is today the Yeonhui-dong neighborhood of Seoul. Ha strongly recommended this site based on its suitability in terms of *pungsujiri* (geomantic principles), but Yi's other lieutenants opposed him. It was not big enough, they said, to build

a palace. They all agreed that even staying in Gaegyeong would be better than building a capital at Muak.

Grudgingly, Yi turned around and left Muak. On his way back, he stopped at Hanyang, formerly the southern Goryeo capital known as Namgyeong. The name Hanyang literally means "north of the Hangang River," and the city, sure enough, was located on a piece of land above the meandering waterway.

After looking around Hanyang, Yi exclaimed:

"This would make a great place for a capital! It's reachable by boat and its central location in the country is ideal."

As soon as he returned to Gaegyeong, Yi issued an order for the relocation of his capital to Hanyang.

That's how, after various ups and downs, Hanyang was chosen as capital of the new state of Joseon. It was picked for the beautiful configuration of its surrounding mountains and rivers, its central position on the Korean Peninsula, and for the ease with which taxes levied in the provinces could be delivered by boat. Taxes in those days were paid in commodities such as rice or fabric, and brought by sea or river to the capital. These deliveries were essential for the state, which could not operate without sufficient tax revenue. Hanyang's advantages as a logistical hub had long been recognized; this is why it had been Goryeo's southern and second capital.

A planned city

On October 25, 1394, Taejo Yi Seonggye left Gaeyeong and arrived in Hanyang. At this point, the latter still had no royal palace and nowhere to house the new government or its many officials. This should give you some idea of how eager Yi was to relocate.

 Muhak Daesa and Joseon's new capital

There are many stories about how Hanyang became the new capital of Joseon. Perhaps the most widely known is that of Muhak Daesa and Wangsimni.

One day, the royal preceptor was out looking for a site to build the royal palace in Hanyang and had found what seemed to be a good spot. Just then, an old man riding past on his cow suddenly shouted out, "Bloody cow! You're as stupid as Muhak!" Startled, Muhak asked the old man where would be a good site for the palace. "Go ten *ri* west of here and you'll find out," the old man replied. Muhak did as he was told, and arrived at the site where Gyeongbokgung Palace now stands. From then

Muhak Daesa
Taejo Yi Seonggye's royal preceptor lived at Hoeamsa Temple in Yangju. Yi trusted him deeply.

on, the place where Muhak had met the old man became known as Wangsimni - it's now a district in eastern Seoul, outside the old city wall.

Another story tells how Muhak Daesa wanted to build the palace in today's Pirun-dong in Jongno-gu Ward, on the eastern flank of Mt. Inwangsan, but was opposed by Jeong Dojeon on the grounds that kings had always ruled from palaces facing south, and that he had never heard of one facing east. Eventually, the palace was built on the site of today's Gyeongbokgung.

Stories such as these, though, are just legends. We have no way of knowing for sure if they're true or not. It seems to me they were created in times of national turmoil, during invasions by the Japanese and the Manchus.

Gyeongbokgung Palace
Joseon's main royal palace was burned down several times over the years due to various wars and disasters. The current structure dates from the rule of Heungseon Daewongun, and was built long after the palace was burned down during the Japanese invasions.

Housed in temporary lodgings, Yi began building his new seat of power. Hanyang was the product of thorough urban planning - a "new town," to use today's term. Unlike the new towns we know, however, it was built not by razing the nearby mountains and filling in waterways to create a geometric grid-like layout, but designed in accordance with the natural topography of the area. This is why the old city today is characterized by meandering curves and round edges rather than straight lines and right angles.

Construction of the capital began with the royal palace. To the people of early Joseon, building a capital meant creating a physical embodiment of an ideal world. At the center of this world was the capital, and at the heart of the capital was the palace: this is why it was the first thing to be built. The palace backed onto Mt. Baegaksan, faced Mt. Namsan and was flanked by Mt. Naksan and Mt. Inwangsan to its left and right, respectively. Today, it is known as Gyeongbokgung.

Gyeongbokgung was named by Jeong Dojeon, the man in overall charge of the building of the new capital. Its name is taken from a line in the classical Chinese poetry collection *Shijing* ("Classic of Poetry") that reads "praying for brilliant blessings." The buildings within the palace, too, have names infused with meaning: the central hall is called Geunjeongjeon, meaning "hall of hardworking government;" the building where the king dealt with most political affairs is called Sajeongjeon, meaning "hall for considering politics;" and the king's sleeping quarters are called Gangnyeongjeon, meaning "hall of eternal tranquility."

The palace was surrounded by a wall, punctuated by gates with meaningful names of their own. The main gate in the eastern wall is called Geonchunmun, the central "*chun*" (春) character of which is the Sino-Korean word for spring. Its counterpart in the western wall is called Yeongchumun, the "*chu*" (秋) character of which means "autumn." The southern main gate, meanwhile, is called Gwanghwamun; the "*gwang*" (光) character in this name is a Sino-Korean word for "light," associated with summer. The northern gate is named Sinmumun, meaning "gate of outstanding military prowess and courage."

Geonchunmun Gate
This is the palace's eastern gate.

Jongmyo Shrine, Sajik Altar and palaces

People at this time believed that a king must always face south while ruling the country, with a *jongmyo*, or ancestral shrine, to his left and a *sajik*, or altar to the gods of earth and grain, to his right. This arrangement is summed up by the Sino-Korean term *jwamyo usa* (左廟右社), meaning "shrine to the left, altar to the right."

Rites to the spirits of the ancestors of the Joseon royal family were conducted at Jongmyo, while those to the gods of earth and grain, the foundations of the national economy, were held at Sajik. You may have heard characters in Korean historical television dramas, imploring the king to "preserve Jongmyo and Sajik" - the people of Joseon regarded the shrine and altar as the lifeblood of the state and revered them as sacred places.

Sajik Altar
Rites to the gods of earth and grain, the foundations of the national economy, were performed here.

Jongmyo Shrine
Here, rites were conducted to the spirits of deceased Joseon kings and queens. Jongmyo Shrine has been designated a World Heritage Site by UNESCO.

Hanyang city wall and Sukcheongmun Gate
Hanyang's city wall was built in about one year, by some 200,000 commoners drafted from throughout Joseon. Today, only parts of it remain. This photo shows Sukcheongmun, the wall's large northern gate, and the wall extending outward from it on each side. Sukcheongmun's other names include Sojimun and Sukjeongmun.

A large street was built outside Gwanghwamun, the main gate of the palace, with government offices arranged along each side. On the left, from the point of a king facing south - the side where the US embassy now stands - were the State Council (Uijeongbu), the Ministry of Personnel (Ijo), Ministry of Rites (Yejo), Ministry of Taxation (Hojo) and the Capital Bureau (Hanseongbu), in order of increasing distance from the palace. Opposite these - on the side where Sejong Center for the Performing Arts now stands - were the Consolidated Army Command (Samgunbu), the Security Council (Jungchubu), the Office of the Inspector-General (Saheonbu), the Ministry of Defense (Byeongjo), the Ministry of Punishment (Hyeongjo) and the Ministry of Public Works (Gongjo). This thoroughfare became known as Six Ministries Street (Yukjogeori). Back then, of course, it was only around half as wide as today, and certainly not surfaced with anything resembling asphalt.

Once the palace, shrine, altar and government offices

were complete, the new capital's builders began putting up a fortified wall around it. This was an even harder task than building the palace itself. Starting at the peak of Mt. Baegaksan, the wall ran all the way around the capital, measuring some eighteen kilometers in total. Seven tenths of the entire wall were built from earth and the rest from stone. Later, during the reign of King Sejong, the earthen parts were replaced with stone. The resulting wall was that which we know today, thanks to the segments of it that remain in northern Seoul neighborhoods such as Samcheong-dong and Seongbuk-dong.

Naturally, the fortress wall also required gates. It had eight of them, four large and four small. The name of each gate incorporated one of the "Five Constants," virtues regarded as important in Confucianism: "*in*" (仁; benevolence), "*ui*" (義; righteousness or justice), "*ye*" (禮; ritual propriety), "*ji*" (智; knowledge) and "*sin*" (信; integrity). The large eastern gate was named Heunginmun, the large western gate Donuimun, the large southern gate Sungnyemun and the large northern

Sungnyemun Gate and signboard
Sungnyemun was Hanyang's main southern gate. After standing unwaveringly in its original form, through a heady succession of wars, for more than six hundred years, Sungnyemun was burned down by an arsonist in February 2008 (left). In May 2013, its restoration was completed.

'Juncheon sisa yeolmudo'
This painting shows the dredging of Cheonggyecheon Stream in the Joseon period, to remove mud and sand from the stream bed and ensure the smooth flow of water. This helped prevent flooding and stop the water from stagnating and growing smelly. Since it flowed through the heart of Hanyang before entering the Hangang River, the state placed great importance in keeping the stream properly dredged.
– Kyujanggak Institute for Korean Studies

gate Sojimun (or Sukcheongmun). Another meaning of "*sin*" is "center," but since there was no place for a gate in the center of the city they built a bell tower, hung an enormous bell in it, and called the structure Bosingak. The sound of the pealing bell spreading out from this location signified the sound of the centre spreading out to the furthest corners of the country. Amazing, isn't it, how a single name can carry such philosophical meaning?

Unjongga and Cheonggyecheon

Joseon's capital, of course, needed not just a palace, a shrine, an altar and government offices but also houses and shops for its citizens. While the fortress wall went up around the city, houses were being built, and roads laid and lined with shops.

A long, straight road was created along a north-south axis from Gwanghwamun, the main gate of Gyeongbokgung Palace, all the way down to Sungnyemun, the city's main southern gate. Another was laid at right angles to this one, running from Heunginmun, the eastern gate, to Donuimun, its counterpart in the west. This second street was lined with shops on both sides and named Unjongga. The "*un*" in this name corresponds to the Chinese character for cloud (雲), which was surely a reference to the cloud-like swarms of people that filled Unjongga with their busy commerce. Today, this street is named Jongno.

A little to the south of Unjongga, a stream named "Gaecheon" flowed through the city, serving as both a place to wash clothes and a sewer. It was formed by rivulets flowing down from the mountains around the city as they came together on their way to larger Jungnangcheon Stream, then into the Hangang River. Gaecheon was originally a natural stream but had been diverted by human intervention to follow an almost entirely straight line. This was the waterway we know today as "Cheonggyecheon," a name acquired during the Japanese colonial period.

Though it's a picturesque stream once again today, the Cheonggyecheon I grew up with was covered over by asphalt and a busy elevated expressway running between rows of apartment blocks. The expressway was built around 1960, when I was born. In 2005, the stream was restored to its former status.

Different status, different neighborhood

Now it was time to build housing. Residential land was

Bukchon today
Yangban aristocrats and high-ranking officials lived near Gyeongbokgung Palace, to the north of Cheonggyecheon Stream. This photo shows today's neigborhood of Gahoe-dong, which forms part of Bukchon Hanok Village. Scenes like this give us some idea of what Bukchon looked like in the Joseon era.

allocated by the state. Senior ministers of the first rank were granted thirty-five *bu*, those of the second rank thirty *bu* and so on downwards with five *bu* fewer for each rank until the sixth, which received ten. Commoners were granted two *bu*. The *bu* was a unit of land area and harvest volume that covered roughly 100 square meters.

Each neighborhood was inhabited by people of different social status. High-ranking officials lived to the east of Gyeongbokgung Palace, in the area known today as Bukchon. Eunuchs lived to the west of the palace, as their jobs demanded that they live close by. This is the area now called Hyoja-dong.

Land to the north of Cheonggycheon Stream was generally inhabited by *yangban* aristocrats, particularly high-ranking officials, while that to the south was principally home to commoners. Between these, on land close to the stream itself, lived those of middle-ranking status such as physicians, interpreters and court painters. Because they lived in the "middle" like this, those of such social status came to be known as *jungin* (literally "middle people"). Merchants, meanwhile, tended to live near the many shops that lined Unjongga.

With housing built, the new capital was complete. It was now named Hanseong. At first, almost all of its residents came from Gaegyeong; the previous inhabitants were forced to move out into Gyeonggi-do, the province that surrounds the capital.

How many people lived in Hanseong at the start? Around 100,000. That's less than a hundredth of the population of Seoul today, which is home to more than 10 million, but at the time it was enough to place the Joseon capital among the world's major cities.

Today's Seoul is several times bigger than Hanseong at the dawn of the Joseon period. Perhaps the most striking difference is that land to the south of the Hangang River, the area we know as Gangnam, is now part of the city. As recently as the 1970s, this was still part of Gyeonggi-do Province and consisted of nothing but rice paddies and dry fields. Oh, and you may be wondering when Hanseong became known as Seoul: after being called Gyeongseong during the Japanese colonial period, the city acquired its current name upon national liberation in 1945. Seoul is a pure Korean word that simply means "capital."

?!

Why the king kept moving palace

Gyeongbokgung was not Joseon's only palace. There were several others, including Changdeokgung, Changgyeonggung, Gyeonghuigung and Gyeongungung. Why? Because the king, rather than staying in one palace, moved around from one to the next. Kings would change palace every few years: Jeongjo, for example, moved every five years, while Gyeongjong moved every single year. So why did monarchs relocate like this so often? Were they looking for somewhere bigger and better to live?

No. Sometimes they moved because of specific events such as fires or outbreaks of disease, but the main reason was political. Just like relocating the capital, moving palace was a way for the king to distance himself from political opponents and create a fresh climate in the royal court, placing himself back at the center.

Gyeongbokgung was Joseon's first and best-known palace, but kings didn't live in it for very long. After the palace was burned down during the Japanese invasions, its site remained an overgrown ruin for some 300 years until Joseon regent Heungseon Daewongun had it rebuilt in the nineteenth century. Most kings lived in Changdeokgung following the Japanese invasions.

There were palaces outside the capital, too, used by the king when traveling through the provinces. These are known as *haenggung*. Examples include Onyang Haenggung, used by King Hyeonjong, who suffered from skin disease, on his frequent trips to the hot springs at Onyang, and Hwaseong Haenggung, used by King Jeongjo whenever he visited Hwaseong Fortress in Suwon.

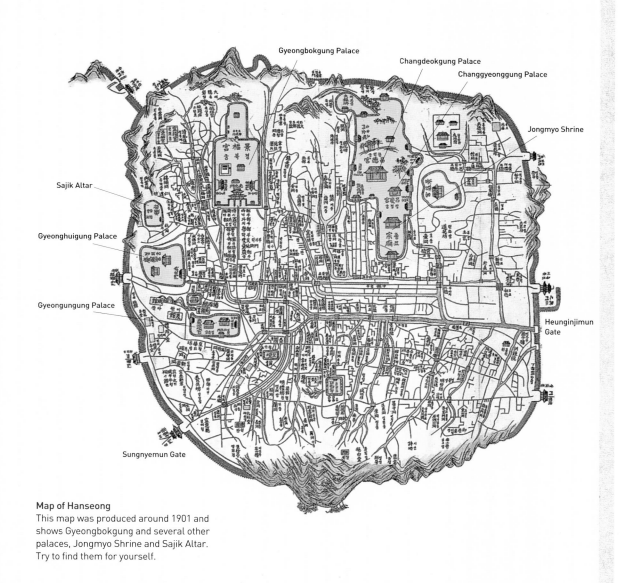

Gyeongbokgung Palace

Changdeokgung Palace

Changgyeonggung Palace

Jongmyo Shrine

Sajik Altar

Gyeonghuigung Palace

Gyeongungung Palace

Heunginjimun Gate

Sungnyemun Gate

Map of Hanseong
This map was produced around 1901 and shows Gyeongbokgung and several other palaces, Jongmyo Shrine and Sajik Altar. Try to find them for yourself.

CHAPTER 3

The real reason Sejong created Hangeul

"[Hangeul] can be learned in less than half a day by a wise person, and in ten days even by a fool. If Confucian texts are translated using it, commoners will be quite able to read them. Using it to write judicial rulings will also help commoners."

TIME LINE

1392
Joseon period
Yi Seonggye founds
Joseon dynasty

1394
Capital relocated
to Hanyang

1443
Sejong creates
Hunminjeongeum

Who created Hangeul? King Sejong and the scholars of Jiphyeonjeon.

Why? Because they felt sorry for illiterate commoners and wanted independence from Chinese culture.

This is the view of most Koreans today when it comes to the creation of Hangeul, the country's indigenous alphabet, almost 600 years ago. But the story I'm going to tell you today is somewhat different. When you've heard what I have to say about the real reason, compare it with the story you've been told so far and decide which you think is right.

Sejong completed the structure of Joseon, which was still quite a new state during his reign. You could say that if Taejo Yi Seonggye and his successor, Taejong, laid the foundations of Joseon, it was Sejong who built the house that stood on them. Sejong systematically set about creating everything the new state needed, in each field: politics, economics, society, culture and so on. The creation of Hangeul came as part of these efforts.

Well then, let's have a look at Sejong's real reasons for devising the new alphabet.

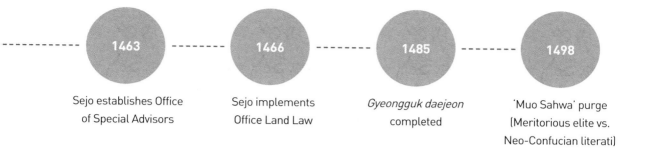

1463
Sejo establishes Office of Special Advisors

1466
Sejo implements Office Land Law

1485
Gyeongguk daejeon completed

1498
'Muo Sahwa' purge (Meritorious elite vs. Neo-Confucian literati)

In 1940, when Korea was a colony of Japan, an old book was discovered in a house in Andong, Gyeongsangbuk-do Province. Opening with the words, "Our language is different from that of China...," this was a copy of *Haeryebon*, an explanation of a new alphabet known at the time as Hunminjeongeum ("Correct Sounds for the Instruction of the People"). *Haeryebon* contained detailed explanations of why Hangeul had been created, the principles behind its design and how it was to be used.

The sudden discovery of this book, lost without a trace for almost 500 years, dispelled all the vague suppositions surrounding the alphabet at the time — that it was modeled after Mongolian 'Phags-pa or an Indian Sanskrit script, or that

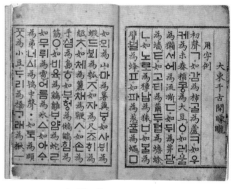

The 'Haeryebon' for Hunminjeongeum
This book explains in detail the reasons for Hangeul's creation and how it should be used.

its angular vowels (ㄱ, ㄴ, ㄷ and so on) were inspired by traditional window paper pasted onto the wooden lattices of windows and doors, for example.

An alphabet to educate the people

Jeong Inji
Sejong appointed Jeong as one of the scholars in Jiphyeonjeon, allowing his talents to flourish. Jeong was a good writer and an outstanding historian, astronomer and musician. Serving seven kings, from Taejong to Seongjong, he left a legacy full of significant achievements.

Haeryebon contains a text written by then-minister of rites, Jeong Inji. In it, he reveals the true reason for the creation of Hangeul:

"If language exists as part of nature, so must script. ... But as all countries apart from China have only languages and no scripts, they borrow Chinese script for their own use. This is like trying to fit a square peg into a round hole and inevitably creates problems."

Jeong also wrote:

"[Hangeul] can be learned in less than half a day by a wise person, and in ten days even by a fool. If Confucian texts are translated using it, commoners will be quite able to read them. Using it to write judicial rulings will also help commoners."

Jeong is saying here that Hangeul was created both to help commoners and to enable them to learn the teachings of Confucianism. This is why the script was originally called Hunminjeongeum.

Let's start by looking at the fact that Hangeul was created to teach the people the tenets of Confucianism. Joseon, unlike Goryeo, took Confucianism as its fundamental ideology. The general public, however, knew nothing about this new thought system. They still believed in Buddhism and led lives steeped in Buddhist culture just as before. What do you expect? Buddhism had played a core role on the Korean Peninsula for almost a thousand years by then. The people of Joseon still gave their dead Buddhist funerals and performed ancestral rites in Buddhist style. In times of trouble they prayed at Buddhist temples.

The state may have changed from Goryeo to Joseon, but its people were just the same as before. The kings of Joseon simply had to do something about this. In order to transform their subjects into "Joseon people," then, they had to teach them about the new ideology and culture.

Do you know what the first book published in Hangeul was? *Yongbi eocheon ga* ("Songs of Dragons Flying to Heaven"). This is a series of long poems, written in Hangeul, that praise the achievements of the founders of Joseon and their ancestors, from Yi Seonggye's great-great-grandfather to King Taejong, and extol the dignity of the new state itself. *Yongbi eocheon ga*

Jiphyeonjeon
Jiphyeonjeon was an academic research institute at the time of King Sejong. This picture shows Sejong himself dropping in to offer its scholars encouragement. Together with the crown prince, other princes and the scholars of Jiphyeonjeon, Sejong set about standardizing the pronunciation of Chinese characters in Korean. In doing so, however, he met with resistance from older and higher-ranking members of the institnte such as Choe Malli.

Sujeongjeon Hall, Gyeongbokgung Palace
Jiphyeonjeon was based in Sujeongjeon Hall. It was here that some of the country's most distinguished scholars gathered to conduct academic research and discuss politics with the king. Like the other buildings of Gyeongbokgung, Sujeongjeon was burned down during the Japanese invasions and rebuilt during the reign of Heungseon Daewongun.

was written in order to make it widely known that the demise of Goryeo and the founding of Joseon were absolutely the right thing.

Strangely, though, *Yongbi eocheon ga* makes no mention of Jeongjong, the second king of Joseon. Why? Did Sejong somehow sneakily push his uncle out of the picture?

From Jeongjong to Sejong, no king of Joseon had been an eldest son. Jeongjong was Taejo's second son, while Taejong Yi Bangwon was Taejo's fifth son and had taken the throne after the abdication of Jeongjong, his elder brother. Sejong, too, became king despite having two older brothers, grand princes Yangnyeong and Hyoryeong. Seen in the context of Confucian principles, which dictated that a monarch had to be succeeded by his eldest son, this presented a serious problem that threatened to undermine the very authority of the king. Sejong's aim, with this in mind, was to reinforce

Joseon's royal authority by emphasizing a line of descent from Taejo to Taejong to himself.

The publication in Hangeul of *Yongbi eocheon ga* was followed by that of other texts, such as *Samgang haengsildo* ("Illustrated Conduct of the Three Bonds"), *Yeollyeodo* ("Illustrated Women of Virtue") and *Hyogyeong* ("Classic of Filial Piety") which contained messages teaching commoners about Confucian virtues such as loyalty, filial piety and chastity. These texts were written in order to familiarize the people of Joseon, who were deeply Buddhist at the time, with the new ideology.

Now, hopefully, you'll understand that Hangeul was created in order to inform the people of the legitimacy of Joseon and to spread the teaching of Confucianism throughout the country. The new alphabet was essential for converting the people of Goryeo into people of Joseon.

Illiterate public: a burden for the king

I mentioned how Hangeul was "a script made for the convenience of the people." But why was it only during

'Samgang haengsildo'
This book explains how to practice the Confucian virtues of loyalty, filial piety and self-restraint. Its illustrations are easy to understand and have explanations above them in Hangeul. Sejong published the book in the belief that the people had to be educated if they were to obey the law.
– National Folk Museum of Korea

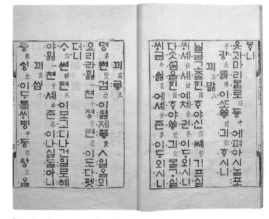

'Worin cheongang-ji gok'
This book, the title of which translates as "songs of the moon's reflections on a thousand rivers," contains hymns written by King Sejong to pray for the peaceful repose of his deceased wife, Queen Soheon, by praising the good deeds of the Buddha.

Sejong's reign that anybody started considering the general public? After all, it had been illiterate throughout the Goryeo period and earlier.

Sejong realized that leaving the people in a state of illiteracy was not in the least helpful when it came to ruling the country. The Mongol invasions and the peasant and *cheonmin* uprisings of the Goryeo period had left them in a state of greater awareness, and the king thought that giving them a way of expressing themselves, and giving himself a way of communicating with them, was necessary for winning them over to his side as he governed.

Sejong regarded teaching his people to read and educating them on the Confucian teachings of loyalty and filial piety as an easy way to better rule his country. He believed this was a shortcut to achieving political stability in what was still a new state.

In that case, couldn't Sejong have simply taught commoners how to read Chinese? By setting up free schools in each village, for example. But that's not what he did. Firstly, learning Chinese characters is very difficult. There was another reason, though: at the time, knowledge of Chinese characters was a clear mark of distinction between the ruling and non-ruling classes. If everybody learned to read and write in Chinese,

'Seodang'
This scene from a *seodang* is by Joseon painter Kim Hongdo. The *seodang* was equivalent to an elementary school today. Chinese was taught here using Hangeul as a tool for learning, with the latter being used to indicate the sound and meaning of each chinese character.
– National Museum of Korea

this distinction would become blurred. This was another factor in the decision to create a separate writing system for the general public.

Was Hangeul created through a collaborative effort?

There was yet another reason for the creation of Hangeul: standardizing the pronunciation of Chinese characters in Korean. At the time, confusion was caused by the use of a variety of sounds; Sejong strongly felt the need to establish a single, fixed pronunciation for each character.

The king's first act after creating Hangeul was to transliterate the Chinese text *Gujin yunhui juyao* ("Abridged Collection of Rhymes Ancient and Modern") into the new script. This was the first step toward standardizing the pronunciation of Chinese characters in Korean. At this time, Hangeul was used as a system of symbols to indicate pronunciation, just as phonetic alphabets are used to indicate pronunciation in an English dictionary.

So why did Sejong want to standardize character pronunciation? An erudite man in various fields, he was a particularly outstanding linguist. If he hadn't become king, he would probably have excelled in this field. Sejong believed that failure to standardize

'Dongguk jeongun' ('Dictionary of Proper Korean Pronunciations') This book was written in order to standardize the pronunciation of Chinese characters, which had previously been in a state of disorder. Its title translates as "proper Korean pronunciation of Chinese characters."
–Konkuk University Sanghuh Memorial Library

the pronunciation of Chinese characters inevitably produced a degree of chaos.

The king put the crown prince — the future King Munjong — in overall charge of the weighty task of standardizing character pronunciation. He also had Prince Suyang, Prince Anpyeong and six scholars from Jiphyeonjeon — Choe Hang, Park Paengnyeon, Sin Sukju, Yi Seollo, Yi Gae and Gang Huian — join the crown prince in his task.

As I said earlier, most Koreans believe Hangeul was created by King Sejong and the scholars of Jiphyeonjeon, working together. That's what school textbooks say, too. In fact, the scholars did not take part in the invention process from the beginning; rather, they joined the project later to write books in the new script once it had been created. And only younger, lower-ranking scholars participated.

When Sejong announced the invention of Hangeul in December 1443 and, two months later, called up young scholars and princes and began standardizing the pronunciation of Chinese characters, the older and higher ranking scholars of Jiphyeonjeon were astonished. Representing himself and six other scholars from the institution, Deputy Minister of Education Choe Malli hastily submitted a petition opposing the new script. After reading the document, Sejong summoned Choe and the other scholars.

"Creating a new script is a discourtesy to Ming and will

reduce us to barbarians," they claimed.

"The ability to make good judgments does not depend upon having a simple writing system."

"The new script is being created too fast and without adequate discussion. The crown prince is absorbed entirely in this project and neglecting his study of Confucianism as a result."

"Transliterating *Gujin yunhui juyao* at will is not right."

But Sejong remained unbowed.

 ### Park Yeon and Jongmyo Jeryeak

Music holds a very important place in Confucianism. Performing rites was a person's duty, while it was music that brought harmony to her or his mind. Music and rites, therefore, were thought to be mutually indispensable.

Jongmyo Jeryeak
This music is performed during ancestral rites to the Joseon royal family at Jongmyo Shrine.

But the music used for rites was different from that enjoyed by the general public. Known as *aak*, it was used when the king and his ministers gathered for morning assembly, for a variety of palace rituals and at national rites. Park Yeon left a tremendously important legacy in standardizing *aak*. He redesigned instruments, arranged scores and established what kind of music had to be used at each kind of ritual. Of the *aak* arranged by Park, Jongmyo Jeryeak and Munmyo Jeryeak, ceremonial music used at Jongmyo Shrine and Munmyo Shrine, respectively, survive today. Munmyo Jeryeak is used for performing rites to Confucius. Nowadays, it has disappeared from China and remains only in Korea.

"I called you here not to reprimand you but to ask you one or two things about your petition. But since you refuse to see reason and keep giving different answers, you leave me little choice but to punish you."

The angry king had Choe and the other six petitioning scholars put in jail, which should give you some idea of how strongly he felt about creating Hangeul. Jeong Changson was sacked from his civil service position, Kim Mun was flogged and the others were later freed. Upon his release, Choe resigned from government, returned to his hometown and died not long afterwards.

A script kept alive by women

Haeryebon was published in September, 1446, two years after Choe Malli and his fellow scholars submitted their petition opposing to the king. Four years later, Sejong died. His ministers praised him for his many great achievements, but neglected to mention the creation of Hangeul.

In the following years, the script failed to find much popularity. Those who considered themselves erudite used only Chinese characters, just as before, while state documents, land deeds and other

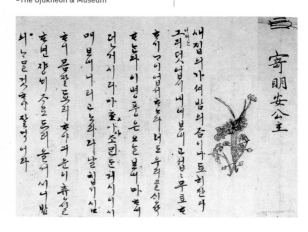

Letter from King Hyeonjong to his daughter
Hyeonjong, eighteenth king of Joseon, wrote this message to his daughter, Princess Myeongan, after she got married and went to live outside the palace. Hyeonjong was very fond of his third daughter, as her two elder sisters had died from illness while still young.
"Are you sleeping well in your new home? I felt so sad after sending you off yesterday, all too soon. Do you miss us? ... Look after yourself in this cold weather... And make sure you eat properly."
–The Ojukheon & Museum

official papers were only recognized if written in Chinese.

Hangeul was used by women, principally the wives of *yangban* aristocrats and court ladies in palaces, in diaries and private letters. It therefore became known as *amgeul*, meaning "women's script."

Leading scholars such as Song Siyeol and Kim Jeonghui would normally write only in Chinese characters, but used Hangeul when writing letters to their daughters or wives. Even kings used the indigenous alphabet rather than Chinese when writing to their daughters.

It seems to me, then, that women preserved and developed Hangeul throughout the Joseon period. If it hadn't been for them, the script may have disappeared altogether.

In the Joseon period, when anyone who wanted to pass the state examination and gain a government position had to master Chinese characters, memorize Confucian texts, and know how to compose poetry in Chinese, it was perhaps natural that Chinese script was considered more important than Hangeul.

Among the general public, however, the number of people using the indigenous alphabet gradually increased. Some began writing political polemics in it and posting them up on walls; other began reading novels written in it. Perhaps it was thanks to the common people that Hangeul kept obstinately alive for so long in spite of so much scorn.

Letter in Hangeul by Queen Inmok
Inmok was the wife of Seonjo, fourteenth monarch of Joseon. This letter contains a get-well message. She penned it in 1603, the year after becoming queen.
– Kyujanggak Institute for Korean Studies

가 나 다 라 마	Seokbo sangjeol
가 나 다 라 마	Neungeomgyeong eonhae
가 나 다 라 마	Worin cheongang-ji gok
가 나 다 라 마	Maengja eonhae
가 나 다 라 마	Daehak eonhae
가 나 다 라 마	Sok myeonguirok
가 나 다 라 마	Oryun haengsildo
가 나 다 라 마	Oryun haengsildo
가 나 다 라 마	Mongyupyeon
가 나 다 라 마	Gungmin sohak dokbon
가 나 다 라 마	Sinjeong simsang sohak

Hangeul printing types
These types were made for printing various books. At the top is a type used to print a work called *Seokbo sangjeol* ("Episodes from the Life of the Buddha"), immediately after the invention of Hangeul; others include fonts used in *Gungmin sohak dokbon* ("People's Elementary School Reader") and *Sinjeong simsang sohak* ("Revised Everyday Elementary School Learning") around 1895.

It was only some 400 years after its creation, at the end of the nineteenth century and when the Joseon period was almost at an end, that Hangeul came to be properly appreciated. Now known as Gungmun ("National Script"), it was used in official documents alongside Chinese characters.

Hangeul became even more widespread during the Japanese colonial period, when foreign occupation made Koreans acutely aware of the value of their own indigenous script. It was during this time, too, that Hunminjeongeum became known as Hangeul ("Korean script"). This name has been widely used since a national Korean language association named the anniversary of the script's proclamation "Hangeul Day."

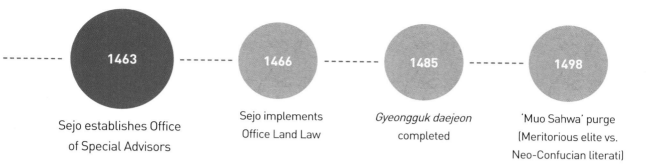

1463	1466	1485	1498
Sejo establishes Office of Special Advisors	Sejo implements Office Land Law	*Gyeongguk daejeon* completed	'Muo Sahwa' purge (Meritorious elite vs. Neo-Confucian literati)

The 'mungwa' examination
Anyone aiming to become a government official had to pass the state examination. You may recall that there was a state examination in the Goryeo period, too. The test was held every two years in Goryeo but only every three in Joseon. This scene in the nineteenth-century painting *Pyeongsaengdo* shows candidates sitting the *sogwa* examination (see p.067).
–National Museum of Korea

The village of Hak-dong in Jeong-eup, Jeolla-do Province, was in the mood for celebration. News had just arrived that one of its villagers, young scholar Park Jingeol, had won first place in the state examination. Park was twenty-four years old. His mother, who had lost her husband at an early age and placed all her hope in her only son, and his wife, who had prayed so hard that he would pass the examination, were almost overwhelmed by the flood of congratulations from other villagers.

Park had come first in the *mungwa* examination. In Joseon, those who wanted to become government officials first had to pass the state examination. Those who succeeded were appointed to government positions according to their examination scores. Joseon officials belonged to one of

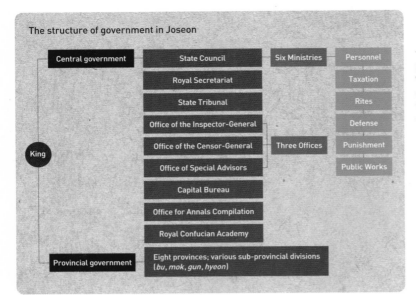

The structure of government in Joseon

The Six Ministries - Personnel, Taxation, Rites, Defense, Punishment and Public Works - were executive organs of government. The Three Offices were those of the inspector-general, the censor-general, and the special advisors.

two categories: civil or military. The former were called *munsin;* the latter as *musin.* Together, both groups were known as *yangban.* The examination used to select civil officials was called the *mungwa*, while that taken by aspiring military officials was the *mugwa.* There was also a third examination, called the *japgwa*, used to select professionals such as interpreters, physicians and jurists.

Some of the most popular professions today, like doctor and lawyer, were regarded as lower in status than civil and military official positions in Joseon. This should give you a sense of how people's attitudes when it comes to profession are not permanently fixed, but change from one era to the next.

Everyone starts at the bottom

Winning first place in the state examination would have

earned Park Jingeol a junior sixth rank position in the civil service. Those who passed were awarded ranks based on their scores: the first-placed candidate would be awarded a junior sixth rank, with others ranked from seventh to ninth in descending order of score.

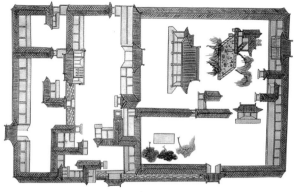

'Hojo gwanado'
The Ministry of Taxation (Hojo), Joseon's equivalent to today's Ministry of Strategy and Finance, was in charge of the nation's economy and finances.

Just as civil service positions in Korea today are divided into grades known as *deunggeup*, those in Joseon were known as *pumgye*. There were nine *pumgye* ranks; each with a senior and a junior level. The descending hierarchy, then, began with senior first rank and ran downwards through junior first, senior second, junior second and so on.

Senior first rank was the highest, while junior ninth was the lowest. The chief state councillor, second state councillor and third state councillor, known collectively as the three councillors, were all of senior first rank. The ministers of

The 'mugwa' examination
Taken by aspiring military officials, this examination did not exist in Goryeo and was introduced in Joseon. This painting shows candidates taking the *mugwa* examination in Gilju, Hamgyeong-do Province.
– National Museum of Korea

'Pumgye' stones
The *pumgye* rankings used in Joseon were similar to the grades used for civil servants today. At morning assembly and various rituals, officials had to stand next to the stone engraved with their rank. These stones are located in the courtyard in front of Geunjeongjeon Hall in Gyeongbokgung Palace. The one in the foreground reads "senior eighth rank."

personnel, taxation and so on were the equivalent of government ministers today and were of senior second rank.

In other words, coming first in the state examination was not a shortcut straight to a high position. Those that achieved it still had to start at junior sixth rank and gradually make their way up to the top.

It was impossible for anyone, no matter how brilliant, to bypass the *pumgye* system or be promoted more than one rank at a time. In order to become a state councillor, anyone starting at junior sixth rank would have to climb, rung by rung, through the fifth, fourth, third and second ranks.

Even the king was unable to disregard *pumgye* rankings and put his favorite men straight into top positions. If he really liked somebody, he could promote him as quickly as possible, but still only one rank at a time. In Joseon, then, it was unthinkable for government ministers to be appointed based on wealth or family background.

Becoming a state councillor was still a distant prospect for Park Jingeol, who had just begun his civil service career. Still, surely it was at least possible if he worked hard. His mother secretly hoped that one day her son would reach the top position.

Let's take a look at what life would have been like for Park as an official of junior sixth rank.

The state examination

There were two types of state examination in Joseon: *singnyeonsi*, held at regular, three-year intervals, and *byeolsi*, announced on an ad hoc basis, at times of national celebration or on other special occasions. A fixed number of officials was appointed after every *singnyeonsi*: thirty-three *mungwa* candidates, twenty-eight *mugwa* candidates and forty-six *japgwa* candidates (nineteen interpreters, nine physicians, nine natural scientists and nine jurists). The number of officials appointed through *byeolsi*, meanwhile, differed each time.

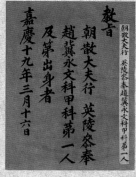

'Hongpae' and 'baekpae' These two certificates were awarded to candidates who passed state examinations: the white *baekpae* certificate went to *saengwon* or *jinsa* and the red *hongpae* to those who passed the *daegwa* of the *mungwa* or *mugwa*. The *baekpae* and *hongpae* in these photographs were awarded to Joseon official Jo Giyeong; the latter indicates that Jo was the highest-scoring candidate. –National Museum of Korea

The *singnyeonsi* was the most important type of state examination, and the most important type within the *singnyeonsi* category was the *mungwa*, which consisted of a preliminary examination called the *sogwa* and a main examination called the *daegwa*. Only those passing the *sogwa* were eligible to take the *daegwa*, while only those passing the *daegwa* could become government officials. Candidates who had passed the *sogwa* were known as *saengwon* or *jinsa*. The *mugwa* also consisted of a *sogwa* and *daegwa*, with those passing the former known as *seondal*.

Excruciating initiation ceremonies

Though he had passed the highly difficult state examination, another imposing hurdle remained for Park Jingeol. Known as the *heochamnye* or *myeonsillye*, this was a hazing ritual at which new officials had to entertain their superiors with food and wine. The ordeal at the hands of superiors was so notorious that some new recruits resigned out of pure fear rather than go through with it. Park braced himself for the ceremony, telling himself it was an inevitable step in the smooth career of an official.

The young recruit was appointed to the Office of Royal Decrees, a government department responsible for recording the content of various documents issued as royal orders. Its *myeonsille* was notoriously harsh. Sure enough, Park had to endure a series of vicious pranks, crying, laughing and rolling in the mud as ordered by his superiors, and having excrement smeared on his face. The game where he had to wear his hat back-to-front, bend over until his head touched the ground and recite the names of official positions was especially hard. The slightest mistake earned him merciless punishment. It was only at daybreak, after spending the night tormenting Park in various ways, that his superiors sang a final song together and disbanded. Park was exhausted but content: finally, he had joined the ranks of his superiors and was truly "part of the family."

Each government department had its own special way of hazing new recruits. Park's friend, Choe Seongho, was appointed as a royal messenger, a type of military official in charge of conveying royal orders and guarding the king. At his gruelling *myeonsillye* ceremony, Choe had to take a deep breath and recite the names of the ten *japsang,* figures placed on the vertical roof ridges of palace buildings to chase away evil spirits, in the correct order, ten times over and in a single breath. If he made a mistake or took a breath before finishing, he had to start all over again.

"Daedangsabu, Sonhaengja, Jeopalgye, Sahwasang, Mahwasang, Samsalbosal, Iguryong, Cheonsangap, Igwibak, Natodu…"

A mistake would have seen him banned from setting foot in the Office of Royal Messengers. Think you could get through a game like that?

Things often went wrong during *myeonsillye*. On one occasion, fire broke out after an attempt to cook some beef. At other times, officials were punished after upturning new recruits and hitting the soles of their feet so hard that the resulting screams reached the ears of the king himself. Less robust recruits sometimes passed out or even died.

Some new recruits bravely refused to attend *myeonsillye*. The famous scholar and politician Yulgok Yi I began his career with a posting to the Bureau of Diplomatic Documents. After refusing a *myeonsillye*, he was eventually kicked out. The

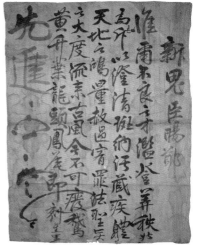

Summons to
an initiation ceremony
"Bring geese, tobacco, pork and chicken immediately and give them to us. From your superiors." The document, signed by three more senior officials, gives a flavor of how new recruits were tormented through *myeonsillye* ceremonies.
–Land & housing Museum

'Japsang' on a palace roof
Japsang are animal- and human-shaped figurines that sit in single file on palace roofs. They are said to drive away evil spirits and prevent disasters. This photo is of the roof of Gyeonghoeru Pavilion in Gyeongbokgung Palace.

069

experience must have left him with a lasting grudge: he later submitted a petition requesting that *myeonsillye* be banned altogether and, upon becoming minister of defense, was at least able to forbid them within his own ministry.

A rigorous selection process

Time went by, and before he knew it Park Jingeol had reached junior second rank. Now, he found himself among the leading candidates to fill the recently vacated post of vice-minister of personnel. Before the Japanese invasions of the 1590s, *munsin* had been appointed by the Ministry of Personnel and *musin* by the Ministry of Defense, but after the wars the Border Defense Council took charge of appointing key officials. This body consisted of the six ministers of state and top military officials, who discussed the most important national policies.

The Border Defense Council appointed officials by way of a highly rigorous procedure. First of all, an official called a *nangcheong* would make the rounds of all members of the council, carrying a piece of paper with their names written on it. Each member would write the names of the candidates he wanted to put forward - generally around three people - on the paper beneath his own name. Recommendations had to be made in consideration of the candidate's professional

'Nangcheong'
These staff officers worked within the Border Defense Council, Tribute Bureau and Five Army Garrisons. They were normally of junior sixth rank, but in some cases ranked as high as senior third or as low as junior ninth. The Border Defense Council employed a total of twelve *nangcheong*: four civil officials of junior sixth rank and eight military officials.

experience, *pumgye* ranking and perceived character; anyone recommending a close personal friend unqualified for the position risked not only incurring harsh criticism but also jeopardizing his own chances of promotion later on.

This method inevitably resulted in certain candidates being recommended multiple times. The individual with the most recommendations would be designated number one candidate, followed by number two, number three and so on, in order of decreasing number of endorsements. The resulting list was known as a *cheonmangdanja*.

Upon receiving the *cheonmangdanja*, the three councillors of state would begin discussing it. Eventually, they would decide on three candidates, usually numbers one, two and three. This final shortlist of three candidates would be presented to the king, who placed a dot above the name of his choice. The number one candidate had the highest chance of being picked, since he was the most widely endorsed.

Kings usually respected the opinions of their ministers wherever possible and picked the candidate recommended by the largest number of them. There was a chance of roughly eighty percent that the king would choose the number one candidate. Though the outcome of the selection process had yet to be revealed, it seemed likely that Park Jingeol would emerge as number one candidate. Despite the suspense, he was doing his best to stay calm.

How were state councillors appointed?

Joseon officials were chosen by way of a prudent and fair process. Gathering the opinions of a number of different people ensured that the right candidate would be chosen for each position. So how were state councillors, the highest officials of all, appointed? Let's have a look at the process, which was known as *boksang*.

Suppose the position of third state councillor was vacant. The king would call the other two state councillors and order them to think of suitable candidates. These two top officials would then select several worthy individuals and recommend them to the king. They would normally recommend three candidates, a process called *sammang*.

Only individuals who met a number of legally defined criteria could be recommended. Firstly, a candidate had to be of senior first rank. Anybody who did not meet this condition, no matter how talented he was or how illustrious his family background, was ineligible. Secondly, he had to have previously headed the Ministry of Personnel and the Ministry of Defense. These were the most important of the six ministries, and anybody who did not know how they operated would be incapable of functioning properly as a state councillor. Thirdly, the candidate had to be somebody that the king did not hold in low esteem. Anybody who didn't perform well at work or wanted in ability was out of the question. Fourthly, the candidate had to have a good reputation among his superiors and inferiors. Anyone lacking the necessary social skills, then, would also be at a disadvantage. In addition, candidates had to be in line with a variety of other legal regulations. In many ways, this appointment process was much more demanding and difficult to get through than any of the requirements for becoming a civil servant today.

The ultimate choice lay with the king, who received the final shortlist of three candidates and selected the one he considered most suitable. Sometimes, however, none of the three names on the shortlist was to the king's liking. If this happened, he would order the two state councillors to come up with new recommendations. Rather than naming any other particular individual, he would merely demand more suggestions. On occasion, this process was repeated several times until the king was finally satisfied.

Once, during the reign of King Sukjong, the position of second state councillor fell vacant. The king summoned the chief state councillor, Kim Suhang, and third state councillor, Yi Danha, and ordered them to recommend candidates for the job. A shortlist was duly prepared, but Sukjong rejected it. Kim and Yi drew up another list, but this one, too, was turned down. After this had happened four times, the two

The chief state councillor's procession
This painting shows a journey by the chief state councillor, the highest-ranking official in Joseon, and his retinue. It is from the picture collection *Pyeongsaengdo*, which depicts the lives of *yangban* aristocrats.
– National Museum of Korea

remaining state councillors requested an audience with the king. After beating about the bush for a while, Sukjong furtively revealed his real reason:

"I know that Jo Saseok, the minister of personnel, is a man who puts everything he has into his job. What do you think?"

Having finally understood the king's intention, the two state councillors quietly went away and drew up another list of candidates that included Jo. The king selected him without hesitation. This should give you some idea of how even the king was unable to handpick his ministers at will and had to follow the same rules and procedures as everybody else.

'Eumseo' and 'cheongo'

Those who wanted to enter government had to pass the state examination. In special cases, however, there were ways that bypassed the examination. These were known as *eumseo* and *cheongeo*. You may recall how *eumseo* also existed in Goryeo. It did not offer access to high positions, however. Those entering the civil service through the *eumseo* system were granted low positions similar to those of candidates who had just passed the state examination; their prospects, meanwhile, were limited and they could not become *dangsanggwan*. As a result, many people avoided *eumseo* from the start, opting to take the state examination instead. Others, meanwhile, began

'Dangsanggwan'
Those of sufficiently high rank to be able to sit in the main hall when leading officials from various departments gathered to discuss political issues were known as In terms of *pumgye*, this meant officials of *tongjeongdaebu* status (senior third rank upwards). *Dangsanggwan* enjoyed the right to vote on matters of utmost national importance, to command the military, and to make personnel appointments.

by taking the *eumseo* path but later sat the state examination as well.

What, then, was the *cheongeo* system? This was a way of appointing hidden men of talent who were well-educated and of virtue. Only one or two people were recruited this way each year in the entire country, and these were generally appointed to a ninth-ranked position known as *chambong*.

So how many government officials were there altogether in Joseon? The number of formal positions, with the exception of temporary and honorary posts, was 2,400. This figure was extremely small in relation to the total population. During the reign of Sejong, for example, Korea was home to around 6.5 million people, so that only around 0.04 percent of the population could have entered public office.

Passing the state examination and becoming a public official, then, was something available only to a small section of the ruling class. Ordinary commoners, toiling in the fields day after day, could only dream of taking the examination. Women and *nobi*, meanwhile, were not even eligible to apply.

Certificate of merit in the founding of Joseon
This document records how, in 1397, Taejo Yi Seonggye officially designated Sim Jibaek a meritorious minister. The descendants of meritorious ministers such as Sim were eligible to obtain government positions by way of the *eumseo* system. In Joseon, far fewer people were eligible to benefit from *eumseo* than in Goryeo. In the former period, the descendants of meritorious subjects and of officials of rank five or above were all able to secure government positions through the system; in the latter, only those of meritorious subjects and officials of rank three and above were eligible.
– Dong-A University Museum

Men of integrity

Hwang Hui, who served as chief state councillor under King Sejong, is revered as one of the most honest officials of Joseon. Known in Korean as *cheongbaengni*, such men were celebrated for being morally upright and untainted by corruption.

Hwang was well known for being not only incorruptible but extremely magnanimous. As such, he is the hero of a number of legends and anecdotes. The following is a typical example: one day, when the peaches on a tree in his garden were just at their ripest and juiciest, a band of children from the village discovered the tree and began scrumping like mad. Rather than scolding them, Hwang, who was reading a book nearby, shouted casually: "I'd like some too, so don't eat them all." When he went outside a little later, however, not a single peach was left.

Bronze statue of Hwang Hui
Hwang, considered one of the most outstanding chief state councillors of Joseon, was renowned for his integrity and magnanimity.

Though he may have been generous and easy-going most of the time, Hwang was stricter than anyone when it came to political affairs. He held the post of chief state councillor for eighteen years, enjoying the full confidence of King Sejong, and was officially designated a *cheongbaengni*.

In Joseon, *cheongbaengni* were rewarded for their honesty and integrity, held up as role models in an attempt to prevent officials being corrupted by money and power. Some individuals were designated *cheongbaengni* during their lifetimes, others after their deaths. Strictly speaking, those chosen while still alive were called *yeomgeumni*, while the term *cheongbaengni* was used for those designated posthumously, but even those originally designated *yeomgeumni* generally became *cheongbaengni* once they had died, so the latter term was often used indiscriminately.

Bangujeong Pavilion
Hwang Hui enjoyed spending time here in retirement. The name Bangujeong literally means "pavilion where the seagulls are your friends." The current structure is a version that was rebuilt after the original pavilion was burned down during the Korean War. It stands by the Imjingang River in Paju. Nearby are a bronze statue of Hwang, his shrine and a memorial hall.

So how were *cheongbaengni* designated? When the king gave an order to pick one, the three state councillors and six ministers would send official documents to all eight provinces, demanding recommendations. Any official could be recommended, but only those of second rank and above could nominate. Candidates put forward by each province would be evaluated before a final choice was made.

Cheongbaengni were designated not according to any fixed schedule but as and when necessary. Sometimes, only one appointment was made in a whole century, while a total of only one or two hundred *cheongbaengni* were designated in the entire Joseon period. How were they rewarded? Those still alive were promoted to a higher rank, while the descendants of those who had died were offered access to government positions as a special privilege.

Most of those designated *cheongbaengni* in Joseon were elderly, high-ranking officials. The Silhak scholar Yi Ik argued that this system of selection was wrong, and that they should be drawn from the lower ranks of the civil service instead.

CHAPTER 5

How did the people of Joseon live?

Farmers required a sound grasp of all the changing seasons and shifting weather throughout the year. If they neglected to do whatever needed doing at just the right time, their crops would fail. From the moment they began plowing the fields, through the transplanting of rice seedlings and weeding to the autumn harvest, there was not a moment's rest to be had. Putting their feet up on public holidays was out of the question. Even in winter, they were kept busy with preparations for the coldest part of the year and for the following spring's farming.

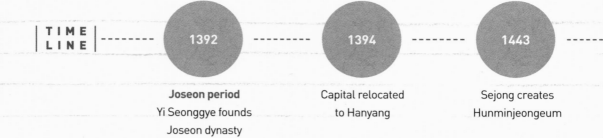

1392
Joseon period
Yi Seonggye founds
Joseon dynasty

1394
Capital relocated
to Hanyang

1443
Sejong creates
Hunminjeongeum

Joseon society was based on a rigid caste system. Social status was hereditary and inescapable, regardless of an individual's talent or ability. A person's life was determined by the identity of her or his parents. Outrageous as this may seem to us today, people at the time accepted it as something natural.

Historically, caste systems were not confined to Joseon but also existed in Europe, Japan, China—almost everywhere, in fact. It was only around 200 years ago that the ideas of universal equality and the abolition of caste systems occurred to anyone.

Life in Joseon varied enormously according to social class. Those born as yangban *were destined to pursue academic study, take the state examination and become officials; those born as peasants were set for a life of work in the fields. Those born as* nobi, *meanwhile, were condemned to serve their masters and mistresses as slaves.*

Let's see how people of each social class lived in Joseon.

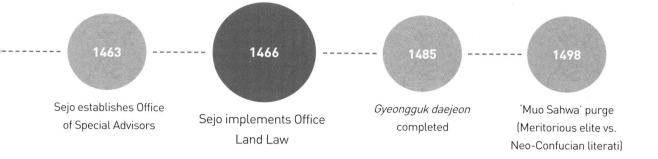

1463	1466	1485	1498
Sejo establishes Office of Special Advisors	Sejo implements Office Land Law	*Gyeongguk daejeon* completed	'Muo Sahwa' purge (Meritorious elite vs. Neo-Confucian literati)

Kim Seonguk, an official at the Office of the Censor-General, was up early and preparing for work. Officials in Joseon had to arrive at work at the time known as *myosi* (from five to seven in the morning), so the first calls from the rooster meant it was time to get going. In winter, at least, they only had to arrive by *jinsi* (seven to nine in the morning).

The Office of the Censor-General, the Korean name of which was Saganwon, was located in what is today the Seoul neighborhood of Sagan-dong, immediately to the east of Gyeongbokgung Palace. Kim rode his horse up Six Ministries Street, past each ministry, turned right in front of Gwanghwamun Gate and rounded the corner of the palace wall to arrive at work.

Six Ministries Street
Every morning, Six Ministries Street, the thoroughfare running due south from Gwanghwamun Gate, filled with officials on their way to work. They commuted in various ways, according to rank: those in sedan chairs would have been among the highest. This photo shows Six Ministries Street in the late Joseon period.
– National Museum of Korea

Hat (above) and civil official's uniform
Joseon's civil officials wore uniforms such as this one, consisting of a hat, a robe called a *dallyeongpo*, a belt around the waist and black boots. *Dallyeongpo* literally means "round-collared robe." The designs on the chest and back of the *dallyeongpo* were called *hyungbae* and varied according to the official's rank.
– National Folk Museum of Korea

Felt hat(right) and military uniform
Military officials in Joseon wore uniforms and felt hats like these. They wore robes called *dongdari*, with sleeves made narrower to aid movement, on top of which they added battle dress. To top it all off, they donned felt hats like this one.
– National Folk Museum of Korea

A day in the life of official Kim Seonguk

The first thing an official did after arriving at work was sign his name in the attendance register. The number of days of attendance was reflected in his appraisal and could affect his chances of promotion — who would want to miss out on promotion by not turning up to work?

Today, there was no morning assembly so Kim had headed straight to the Office of the Censor-General. On days when morning assembly was held, he would have first gone to the palace. Morning assembly was a gathering at which all officials paid their respects to the king. They would dress in their official robes and assemble in front of the main palace hall to greet him. On such days, officials had to get up even earlier, since assembly took place at *insi* (three to five in the morning), before regular working hours.

You will have worked out by now that being an official was not a job well-suited to lazy people. This was natural: how could anyone entrusted with the huge responsibility of managing the politics and economy of the state afford to be idle?

There were three types of morning assembly: *joha*, which took place on the first and fifteenth day of every month; *jocham*, which was held on the fifth, eleventh and twenty-first days; and finally a daily assembly called *sangcham*. The latter was attended only by *dangsanggwan* from key departments such as the State Council, the Six Ministries, the Capital Bureau, the Office of the Inspector-General, the Office of the Censor-General and the Office of Special Advisors. Kim Seonguk himself would probably have attended a morning assembly every four or five days. Luckily, there were times when scheduled assemblies were canceled. On such occasions, Kim secretly relished his extra couple of hours' sleep.

The Office of the Censor-General was responsible for keeping government policy on the right track, giving the king warnings and advice when necessary, and monitoring other officials to prevent corruption. Working there required courage and the resolve to resign if the king failed to heed a warning. After Kim got to work each morning, his day was a busy one.

Before he knew it, it was time to go home. Work normally finished at *yusi* (five to seven in the evening), but this was brought forward to *sinsi* (three to five) in winter. In other words, officials worked for eight hours a day in winter and twelve hours the rest of the year: much longer than civil servants these days.

What did officials do after work? Sometimes they would get together with colleagues from the same department,

Plowing
This painting by Kim Hongdo shows farmers breaking apart clods of earth as they plow a paddy.
– National Museum of Korea

Rice planting
These farmers are hard at work planting rice. Behind them is a woman carrying a basket, no doubt full of tasty lunch, on her head.
– Dong-A University Museum

and sometimes they would meet friends or relatives. There was no equivalent to today's Sunday; rather, days off came in the form of national holidays or on the dates of royal ancestral rites. National holidays included the king, queen and queen mother's birthdays and festivals such as Seol (Lunar New Year) and Chuseok (Harvest Festival). Royal ancestral rites, of course, were held on the anniversaries of the deaths of kings and queens. On days off, officials would go the archery field with their friends for some target practice, or head off to a scenic spot and relax.

A day in the life of farmer Yi Makdong

Just as the sun was poking its head above the horizon, Yi Makdong made his way to his paddy field. He walked quickly, in a hurry to finish off the plowing he hadn't managed to get done the day before.

Once he had been working for some time, the sun reached the top of the sky. As if on cue, he saw his wife approaching with a basket on her head. She had been beautiful when they married, but now her face was tanned almost black by the sun and covered in fine wrinkles.

"I'll buy her a nice comb from the market if I work hard enough and get a good harvest this year," he muttered to himself.

His wife's basket contained a mixture of rice and barley and some wild shoots and leaves. It was the food of a poor household, but tasted divine after a long morning of sweaty work in the field. Yi got back to work. Only when the sun began to set did he finally stop working and return home.

Farmers required a sound grasp of all the changing seasons and shifting weather throughout the year. If they neglected to do whatever needed doing at just the right time, their crops would fail. From the moment they began plowing the fields, through the transplanting of rice seedlings and weeding to the autumn harvest, there was not a moment's rest to be had. Putting their feet up on public holidays was out of the question. Even in winter, they were kept busy with preparations for the coldest part of the year and for the following spring's farming.

Yi thought back to when he had read the barley roots at Ipchun, the first day of early spring according to the twenty-four traditional seasonal divisions. It was believed that these roots, when dug up at Ipchun, could be used to divine what lay ahead for that year's farming: three or more roots signaled a bumper harvest, while a single root spelled a lean year. Two roots, meanwhile, suggested an average harvest was on the way. That spring, the barley he dug up had shown him three roots: a positive sign, to be sure.

"This'll be a good year," Yi muttered to himself as he lay down. "No doubt about that." He was asleep before he knew it.

A day in the life of the king

The monarch began his day by greeting his mother and grandmother. He had to get up before daybreak and put on a smart set of clothes before going to meet them. If he was unable to go in person, he had to send a eunuch to deliver his greeting instead.

As the sun began to rise, it was time for *gyeongyeon*, a session at which the king discussed academic issues and politics with his ministers. Only after *gyeongyeon* did he get a chance to have breakfast. This was followed by morning assembly, after which he received reports from his ministers on their work. These reporting sessions were attended at all times by official historians,

The king's duties
Every day for the king was a busy one. His schedule was crammed full, from morning to evening. Here, we see a minister giving him a progress report while an official historian writes down what is said.

whose task it was to listen to and record what was reported to the king.

Once the reporting session was over, a line formed of officials waiting to convey various bits of information from their respective departments to the king. By the time they were all done, it was *osi* (eleven in the morning to one in the afternoon). After a quick lunch, the king was off again to attend *jugang*. Like *gyeongyeon*, this was a gathering with ministers for study and discussion.

After *jugang*, the king received ministers leaving the capital to serve in provincial administrative positions, and those returning from the provinces. At this gathering, he urged the former to take proper care of the people, and heard reports from the latter of difficulties faced in the regions and offered solutions.

One thing the king had to be sure to do at *sinsi* (three to five in the afternoon) was check the list of soldiers was check the list of soldiers on guard and ministers on late duty in the palace that night, and decide on a new password. These were very important tasks when it came to his own safety.

Before dinner came *seokgang*, the evening study session. In other words, the king studied three times every day. Only after he had eaten dinner did he finally have time to relax a little.

Still, there were other things to be done first. When he thought of the people all over the country waiting patiently for him to deal with their problems, there was no way he could contemplate being lazy. The last thing he did before going to bed was bid good night to his elder relatives in the palace.

The king's day was only over once he had done all of these things. Being number one in the kingdom was no piece of cake.

A day in the life of Mandeugi the 'nobi'

The life of a 'nobi'
Can you see the female *nobi* on the left of this picture? She lives in the home of her master, performing housework. The boy on the right with plaited hair is another *nobi*, running an errand.
–National Museum of Korea

Mandeuk was eleven years old. He had been a *nobi* from birth, as this was the status of both his parents. His father was attached to a government department, while his mother worked in the home of a higher-class mistress. *Nobi* working in government offices were called *gwannobi*, while those attached to private households were known as *sanobi*.

Mandeuk began each day by fetching water for his master to wash. The latter was a government official who rose before daybreak, which meant that Mandeuk had to get up even earlier. He would clear away his master's bedding,

People at work
Joseon society had a rigid caste structure; an individual's work was determined by social status. This Joseon-era folk painting shows an autumnal scene.
– National Museum of Korea

tidy the room, fetch shoes and then go on to do countless other small errands.

Mandeuk had another important duty, too: looking after Sukgeon, his master's only son. Sukgeon was three years younger than Mandeuk, but he was such a bundle of mischief that Mandeuk couldn't afford to let him out of his sight for

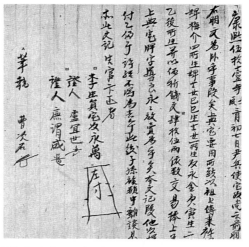

Bill of sale for two 'nobi'
Since *nobi* were regarded as the property of their master, they could be bought or sold at the will of the latter. This document records the sale of two *nobi* for forty-five *nyang*. –National Museum of Korea

even a moment. The boy's father flew into a rage whenever Sukgeon hurt himself or cried, so Mandeuk had no choice but to follow him around all day long.

One day, Sukgeon got his face scratched by the neighbors' cat. It was his own fault for tormenting the creature until it snapped, but Mandeuk was the one who got a thrashing from the master that night for not

 How 'baekjeong' became 'cheonmin'

The term "*baekjeong*," used in Joseon for butchers, had originally been used in Goryeo to refer to ordinary peasants. In Goryeo, butchers were called *yangsucheok* or *hwacheok*. So why did the word *baekjeong* acquire a different meaning in Joseon?

In Joseon, too, the term *baekjeong* referred for quite some time to ordinary peasants. During the reign of King Sejong, however, the status of *yangsucheok* and *hwacheok* was raised to become equal to that of *baekjeong*. This was done for reasons of taxation: at the time, it was ordinary peasants that paid tax. The greater the number of peasants, or baekjeong, the more tax could be levied and the richer the state became.

When the statuses of *yangsucheok* and *hwacheok* were elevated to that of *baekjeong*, the original *baekjeong* - ordinary peasants - grew angry. They resented being put in the same social category as butchers, who had previously been regarded as untouchables by the rest of society. They therefore began resenting and looking down upon the term *baekjeong* itself. Eventually, ordinary peasants became known by other terms, such as *baekseong*, *pyeongmin*, *yangmin* and *chonmin* instead of *baekjeong*, while latter term became associated exclusively with butchers.

looking after Sukgeon properly. Not that there was anything unusual about this: sometimes, he even got flogged for failing to catch Sukgeon when the boy fell over.

Mind you, the master didn't always take Sukgeon's side. Once, while Mandeuk was eating dinner, Sukgeon summoned him to the outhouse. Mandeuk immediately stopped eating and ran to answer the call. Seeing this, Sukgeon's father gave him a harsh telling off. No master should ever call a servant to the outhouse while he's eating, he said.

As he lay down to sleep that night, Mandeuk secretly looked forward to the day when Sukgeon grew up and he no longer had to follow him everywhere.

Joseon: a class-based society

Like that of Goryeo, Joseon society was based on a caste system. It comprised four social classes: *yangban*, *jungin*, *sangmin* and *cheonmin*. Meanwhile, some scholars maintain that it was divided into just two classes: *yangin* and *cheonin*. More research is needed before we can prove for certain who's right. In my opinion, though, the four-way division into *yangban*, *jungin*, *sangmin* and *cheonmin* is probably closer to the reality of the time.

The *yangban* class included civil and military officials, their families and their relatives. *Jungin* were professionals such as

Family registers and 'hojudanja'
Family registers were rewritten every three years. The head of the household would write down all the necessary information, such as his job, age and family members, and submit it to a government office. Officials would then create a family register based on these details. The form submitted by the head of the household was known as a *hojudanja*. Those who needed extra official copies of their register could obtain them from government offices, just as similar offices provide official copies of citizen's identity cards today. Such official copies were called *junhogu*.

– Museum of Old Roads

'Hopae'
Nowadays, all citizen's identity cards are of the same format, but *hopae*, their equivalents in Joseon, differed according to social status. *Yangban* had *hopae* made of ivory or horn, while *sangmin* versions were carved from wood.

– National Museum of Korea

interpreters, physicians, jurists and painters. *Sangmin* were principally peasants, while the ranks of *cheonmin* included *nobi*, *baekjeong* and entertainers.

Yangban enjoyed tax exempt status. *Nobi* didn't pay taxes, either; rather, they were treated as "living tools" and regarded as the property of their owners. It was *sangmin* who paid taxes.

People in those days carried around identity tags, called *hopae*, with a similar function to the citizen's identity cards held by Koreans today. Each *hopae* was engraved with the name, year of birth, position and social class of its bearer. These tags differed in appearance according to social class. Those carried by *yangban* were made of ivory or horn, while those of *sangmin* were made of wood. Of course, photography hadn't yet been invented so a *hopae* bore no image of its owner.

Family registers like those used by Koreans today existed in Joseon. At the time, they were created in order to ensure accurate taxation. Re-written every three years, these registers recorded the place of residence, occupation, class, name, age, family clan and previous four generations of ancestors of the head of the household, as well as the surname, age, and previous four generations of ancestors of his wife, and the names and ages of all his children. The names of any *nobi* working in the household were also recorded.

Joseon's children

Today, nine-year-old Subong went out to play without studying again. Unable to put up with his behavior any longer, his grandfather smacked him five times on the back of his head and four times on his bottom. Su-bong lay face-down on the ground, sobbing, a sight that left his grandfather feeling quite cut up. That evening, the old man wrote a poem full of warm feeling for his grandson.

No young boy could study all day,
but I just wish you would use your life wisely.

I quietly scold you, but still you don't listen.
You go off running around with other children at every chance.

When I send a servant to fetch you, you hover outside the gate, scared of coming in for another telling-off.

I drag you inside, smacking you on your head and your behind.
But it breaks my heart when you lie down and cry afterwards.

This story is found in *Yanga rok* ("Record of Raising a Child"), a diary kept by scholar and former high-ranking official Yi Mungeon as he

Catching dragonflies
This late-Joseon folk painting shows children waving butterfly nets around to try and catch dragonflies.
- National Folk Museum of Korea

raised his grandson, Subong. Like Subong, all Joseon boys born into *yangban* families had to learn classical Chinese and study Confucian texts. Later, when they were grown up, they would have to take the state examination. It seems children then and now are just the same in preferring to play rather than study.

Girls did not study classical Chinese or Confucian texts. Instead, they learned domestic skills such as sewing, cooking and weaving and the knowledge needed to become industrious, thrifty and virtuous wives. Let's have a look at what girls were taught:

To be composed, considerate, submissive and diligent.

To perform ancestral rites with solemnity.

To show respect and affection to their parents-in-law.

To serve their husbands with courtesy.

To educate their children with a proper sense of duty.

To respect and warmly receive relatives.

To weave diligently.

To be frugal with money.

Once boys and girls reached the age of fifteen or sixteen, they were regarded as adults and got married.

CHAPTER 6

Joseon,
land of Confucianism

Hopefully you'll understand by now that Seo Gyeongdeok, Yi Hwang, Jo Sik and Yi I were all leading Joseon Neo-Confucian scholars but all had slightly different philosophies of their own, and that each lived differently according to his personal circumstances and character. If Seo in some ways resembled a Taoist immortal, at one with nature, Yi Hwang was like a lofty, solitary pine tree growing high up on the side of a sheer cliff. Jo was as pure as the wind sweeping over a mountaintop, while Yi I was like the full moon shining down onto a lake.

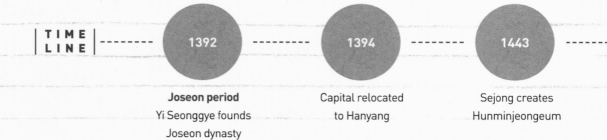

TIME LINE

1392
Joseon period
Yi Seonggye founds
Joseon dynasty

1394
Capital relocated
to Hanyang

1443
Sejong creates
Hunminjeongeum

Goryeo was a Buddhist country. Joseon, by contrast, took Neo-Confucianism as its basic ideology. Just like the saying, "New bottles for new wine," the new state needed a new ideology.

Wait a minute, you might say. I thought Joseon's main ideology was Confucianism, not Neo-Confucianism. What's the difference? Well, the latter is one branch of the former. As the name suggests, it's a re-interpreted version of Confucius's original ideology and It can be seen as falling within the framework of Confucianism in its widest sense. In other words, both notions are correct: broadly speaking, the basic ideology of Joseon was Confucianism; in a more precise sense, though, it was Neo-Confucianism.

After originating in China, Neo-Confucianism reached the Korean Peninsula in the late Goryeo period. Here, it was warmly welcomed by the members of the reformist New Gentry faction who dreamed of change and found the new system of thought truly fresh and idealistic. When Joseon was founded, the New Gentry took Neo-Confucianism as their fundamental ideology and started applying its principles to everyday life.

Let's take a closer look at what Neo-Confucianism actually is, and how it spread its way among the people of Joseon.

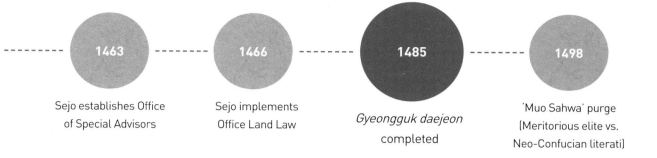

1463 Sejo establishes Office of Special Advisors

1466 Sejo implements Office Land Law

1485 *Gyeongguk daejeon* completed

1498 'Muo Sahwa' purge (Meritorious elite vs. Neo-Confucian literati)

The early years of the sixteenth century, around 100 years after the founding of Joseon, saw the emergence of several truly outstanding scholars who laid the basis for the establishment of Neo-Confucianism in the country. These were Hwadam Seo Gyeongdeok, Toegye Yi Hwang, Yulgok Yi I and Nammyeong Jo Sik. The Joseon period as a whole produced many other scholars just as brilliant as these four, but the reason I mention them here is that they were more or less contemporaries, making it interesting to draw comparisons between them. Let's compare the lives of these Neo-Confucian scholars while we consider the true nature of their common ideology.

Seo Gyeongdeok's unique study technique

Seo is famous for an anecdote in which he stars alongside the famous *gisaeng* Hwang Jini. Hwang admired Seo's deep erudition and became his student. One day, she spoke to him:

"We have three outstanding things here in Songdo."

"And what are they?"

"Bagyeon Waterfall, you and me, Jini."

Seo roared with laughter.

Seo was born in Songdo in 1489, during the reign of King Seongjong—you will hopefully recall that Songdo was another name for Gaegyeong, the Goryeo capital.

Though he did pass the state examination, Seo never entered public office. He learned by himself, without a teacher. Seo's way of studying was highly unusual: he would take a single philosophical subject and mull it over and over in his head until he had a complete grasp of it. They say he used this technique from a young age.

One day, when Seo was just a young boy out picking wild herbs, he came across a skylark. "Why on earth does the lark keep popping in and out of its nest?" he wondered to himself. "Why has it built its nest at the top of that tall tree?" "Why does it keep on and on singing?" "And why does it flap its wings that way?" Lost

'Hwadamjip'
This book contains the collected writings of Seo Gyeongdeok. Hwadam was Seo's pen name. His mother is said to have given birth to him after a dream in which she entered a shrine to Confucius. Perhaps her dream portended well, since Seo went on to become a brilliant Confucian scholar.

Bagyeon Waterfall
This waterfall lies sixteen kilometers north of Gaeseong. Along with scholar Seo Gyeongdeok and *gisaeng* Hwang Jini, it is known as one of the "Three Beauties of Songdo."

in all these thoughts, he dropped the herb basket on the ground and spent the whole day watching the lark.

Even once he reached adulthood, Seo would write the name of a particular object, stick it on the wall and then kneel down in front of it for days on end, immersed in thought, until he had worked out the logic behind it. One day, he wrote down the word "wind," stuck it up on the wall and spent the whole day contemplating it; another day, he posted up the word "fan" and considered the reason a fan produces a cool breeze. If anyone asked him why he was kneeling down like this, he would answer that that was the only way for his mind to become unified, and that studying without a unified mind stopped his thoughts unfolding properly.

One of the things Seo mastered through this unusual

Yi Jiham and 'Tojeong bigyeol'
This Joseon period map is called *Gyeonggangbu imjindo*. Mapo, where Yi Jiham lived, is marked as Tojeong. This place name was directly derived from Yi Jiham's pen name. Yi built himself an earthen dugout hut at Mapo and lived there. He therefore gave himself the pen name Tojeong, literally meaning "earthen dugout." His work, *Tojeong bigyeol*, is known today as a book of fortune telling, but was originally written to give a sense of hope to the poor commoners living near the ferry crossing at Mapo.
– Kyujanggak Institute for Korean Studies

technique was the philosophy of *gi* ("energy"). He claimed that all things in the world were formed by *gi*, and that *gi* was not fixed but in a constant state of flux. He believed that this also applied to life and death, so that there was no beginning and no end and everything was in an endless state of continuity. When Seo was approaching death, at the age of fifty-eight, his students asked him:

"Master, how do you feel?"

"I worked out the principle of life and death long ago," he replied. "So I feel quite relaxed."

These words are a good illustration of Seo's philosophy.

Though Seo was self-educated and had no teacher of his own, he taught a great number of students. The best-known among them was Yi Jiham, author of *Tojeong bigyeol* ("Secrets of Tojeong"; Tojeong was Yi's pen-name).

Yi Hwang and Jo Sik, the two Neo-Confucian scholars of Yeongnam

In 1501, twelve years after the birth of Seo Gyeongdeok, Toegye Yi Hwang and Nammyeong Jo Sik came into the world. These two men provide many interesting points of comparison with each other. Not only were they born in the same year; they both came from Gyeongsang-do Province, too.

Yi Hwang was born in Ongye-ri in Yean-hyeon (today's Dosan-myeon in Andong City, Gyeongsangbuk-do Province), while Jo Sik was born in Samga-hyeon (today's Hapcheon in Gyeongsangnam-do Province). As the Nakdonggang River wound its way south towards the sea, Yi Hwang lived to the east of it in Yean and Jo Sik to the west of it in Samga. People at the time therefore used to say that Yi led the left side of Yeongnam and Jo the right side (Yeongnam is a name often used for the southeastern region comprised of today's Gyeongsang provinces, while the left-right division was based on a perspective facing south from the capital).

Both men were leading Neo-Confucian scholars of their era, but each of them followed a different path. Jo Sik never took on a government position, instead concentrating solely on educating his students. Yi Hwang, by comparison, passed the state examination at the age of thirty-four and subsequently spent his career in various major and minor official positions until his retirement at the age of sixty. Yi resigned several times but was always summoned again by the royal court. Only when he reached sixty did he leave public office altogether, return to his hometown, found Dosan Seowon

Dosan Seowon
Located in Andong, Gyeongsangbuk-do Province, this *seowon* is where ancestral rites to Toegye Yi Hwang are now held. The *seodang*, where Yi taught his students, is located at the back of the complex. Dosan Seowon became a center of Confucian study, frequented by Confucian scholars throughout the rest of the Joseon period.

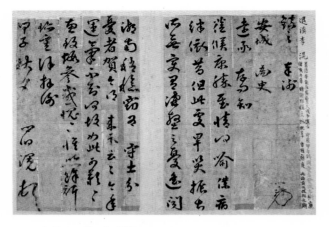

Letter written by Yi Hwang
This letter was sent by Yi to a friend as a Chuseok greeting. In it, the philosopher describes how a severe drought that year has left many peasants starving and how he himself is sick. He also thanks the friend for a gift.
– National Museum of Korea

and immerse himself in study and teaching.

For the next ten years, Yi studied Neo-Confucianism. When he died, at the age of seventy, he left a highly valuable legacy. His death was a rather unusual event, reflective of his profound philosophical accomplishment. After watering his beloved plum tree and tidying his bed, he sat in a completely upright position and simply stopped breathing. Jo Sik, too, died around one year after Yi.

Yi and Jo lived at a time when politics in Joseon was dominated by Queen Regent Munjeong and her younger brother, Yun Wonhyeong. Munjeong stopped at nothing when it came to increasing the wealth and honor of her clan and herself, while Yun and other members of her family engaged in all manner of corruption, confident in the queen's protection.

Jo was harshly critical of this corruption and considered himself unable to even set foot in the royal court while it was infested with such people. This is why he refused to take on an official position and devoted himself to teaching his students. Jo and Yi exchanged several letters, in which Jo quietly reproached Yi for serving such a dirty royal court.

While both Jo and Yi were critical of political realities, their

Sancheonjae and Jo Sik
Jo built this village school in Sancheong, in view of Mt. Jirisan. He never worked in government, concentrating instead on educating his students.

studies of Neo-Cofucianism took slightly different directions. Yi regarded *i* (principle) as constituting the basis of all things. In contrast to Seo Gyeongdeok's ever-changing vital force, *gi*, Yi's *i* was fixed and immutable. Yi studied Neo-Confucianism in great depth, focusing on *i*.

Jo Sik emphasized practice over theory. "Other scholars have already eluciated the intentions of the great sages," he would say to his students. "So scholars today should worry not about lacking knowledge but about how to implement it."

Jo submitted several petitions criticizing problematic aspects of politics and society. In his view, the paramount duty of the educated was to provide accurate and penetrating criticism. Several of his students later became active resistance fighters during the Japanese invasions. One leading example was Gwak Jaeu, the so-called General in Red. In accordance with Jo's teachings, Gwak unhesitatingly took a leading role in the fight to save his country at a time of deep crisis.

Today, Jo Sik is not nearly as well known as Yi Hwang. Why? Because one of his best students, Jeong Inhong, served as a state councillor under Gwanghaegun, the fifteenth king of Joseon. When Gwanghaegun was dethroned, Jeong was branded a traitor and put to death. Though Jo was already dead by this time, the mere mentioning of his name was banned because he had been labeled the teacher of a traitor. This stopped his academic legacy receiving the attention it deserved.

Yi I: born from a dream of dragons

Yulgok Yi I was born in Gangneung, Gangwon-do Province, thirty-five years after Yi Hwang and Jo Sik. His mother was Saimdang Sin, commonly known as Sin Saimdang. She is said to have given birth to Yi I after dreaming that a black dragon of the East Sea came into her home carrying a baby and placed it in her arms. When Yi I was young, therefore, he was often called Hyeollyong, meaning "dragon manifested in the world."

Yi I worked in public office throughout his life, taking an active role in politics. He held a wide variety of high-ranking positions including minister of personnel, minister of defense, minister of taxation and inspector-general. The

Yulgok Yi I and Ojukheon
Yi I was born in the building in the photograph below. Its name, which means "black bamboo house" comes from the abundant black bamboo that grows nearby. A sign over the doorway to the room on the right reads Mongnyongsil, which means "dragon dream room." It was here that Yi's mother, Sin Saimdang, gave birth to him after dreaming of a black dragon. Ojukheon is located in Gangneung, Gangwon-do Province.

scholar was politically active because he lived in a different era to that of Seo Gyeongdeok, Yi Hwang and Jo Sik.

As I've just mentioned, Queen Munjeong and her relatives dominated

the era in which these earlier scholars lived. It was hard, at this time, for men with any moral backbone to endure life in the royal court. After Munjeong's death, however, the situation changed. Their students, rather than living in obscurity, entered service in the royal court. This was the period in which Yi I took an active role in government.

Yi sometimes felt the desire to resign from his position and go to live in tranquility, away from the many complications of court life. But he was dissuaded from quitting by Yi Jiham, his close friend and author of *Tojeong bigyeol*. Jiham had high expectations of his friend and did not want him to leave public office, even though he himself refused to take a government position.

"As long as you're still part of the government, the country at least has some chance of not going completely over the edge," he said.

What, then, were Yi I's intentions while in government? He wanted the country to be ruled for the sake of its people. He emphasized this when speaking to the king:

Yi I's family tombs
Behind Jaun Seowon, where ancestral rites to Yi I are held, lie the tombs of his family. Yi and his wife; his mother, Sin Saimdang; his father, Yi Wonsu; and his sister, Maechang, and her husband, are all buried here. The site is located in Paju, Gyeonggi-do Province.

"There can be no king without a country, and no country without people," he said. "Nothing must matter more to you than your people. But what matters most to them is having enough to eat. If they cannot feed themselves, the whole country will face ruin."

Government for the sake of the people, in Yi I's view, meant providing economic stability so that they had enough to eat. He believed this must come before the teaching of ethics and morals.

Unlike Seo Gyeongdeok, whose thought focused on *gi*, or

The National Code - Neo-Confucian ideology in practice

The most important law in Joseon was called *Gyeongguk daejeon* (the "National Code"). After its initial proclamation in 1469, during the reign of King Seongjong, it was amended several times and finally completed in 1485. The law contains a series of legal articles that embody Neo-Confucian ideology. The following are a few examples:

- The sons of remarried women cannot become government officials.
- The sons of concubines are not eligible to sit the state examination.
- *Nobi* making any accusation against their masters other than treason will be hanged.
- Upon getting married, a bride must move in with the family of her husband.

Aimed at establishing Neo-Confucian morals and social order, these legal regulations had not previously existed. This meant that they were considerably out of line with the sentiments and customs of commoners at the time. It took a long time for everyday Koreans to accept Neo-Confucian ethics and morals as their own.

Yi Hwang, whose philosophy revolved around *i*, Yi I thought of the two as coexistent.

"Anyone who tries to divide *i* and *gi* really hasn't discovered the truth," he said. "And yet, it's hard to understand or explain the wondrous fusion that exists between the two."

Filial piety, loyalty and the Three Bonds and Five Relationships

Hopefully you'll understand by now that Seo Gyeongdeok, Yi Hwang, Jo Sik and Yi I were all leading Joseon Neo-Confucian scholars but all had slightly different philosophies of their own, and that each lived differently according to his personal circumstances and character. If Seo in some ways resembled a Taoist immortal, at one with nature, Yi Hwang was like a lofty, solitary pine tree growing high up on the side of a sheer cliff. Jo was as pure as the wind sweeping over a mountaintop, while Yi I was like the full moon shining down onto a lake.

But what actually are the *i* and *gi* that these men spent so much time talking about?

Since the distant past, people have wanted to understand the origins of the universe. Philosophy was born out of this curiosity. Some Western philosophers considered water or fire to lie at the root of all things. Neo-Confucianism, an

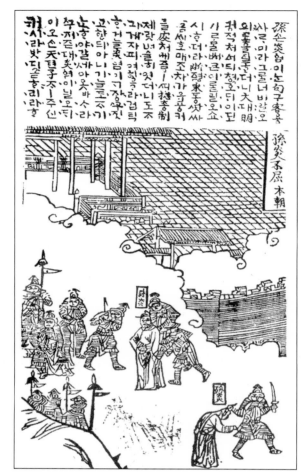

Loyalty and filial duty as depicted in Sok samgang haengsildo ('Illustrated Conduct of the Three Bonds, Continued') This book was published in order to encourage the people of Joseon to embody the principles of loyalty and filial piety. While *Samgang haengsildo* ("Illustrated Conduct of the Three Bonds") mainly featured Chinese protagonists, *Sok samgang haengsildo* starred Korean characters. The page on the left describes how Son Yeom, a loyal subject, was caught by enemies but refused to surrender, eventually paying for his loyalty with his life. The right-hand page shows dutiful son Seo Man knocking a hole in the ice on a freezing winter day in order to feed his sick father, whereupon four fish jump out of the water.

Eastern philosophy, explained the cosmos by way of the fundamental concepts of *i* and *gi*. *Gi* is that which moves all things, while *i* is the basis of *gi*. When applied to people, *gi* becomes human instinct and *i* becomes morality. In embodying morality, people must remain faithful to *i*. The specific details of such practical embodiment are known as the Three Bonds and Five Relationships.

Among the Three Bonds and Five Relationships, filial piety is the most important of all, constituting the fulfillment by every person in society - king, minister, commoner and so on - of her or his proper duties. In the case of peasants, these duties comprised working hard in the fields, looking after parents and paying tax to the state. When it came to relationships vis-à-vis the king, filial piety became known as loyalty.

In Neo-Confucianism, loyalty and filial piety were two sides of the same coin, both important principles in holding together the class-based society of the age. Are you confused yet? It gets more complicated, but let's stop here for now. I myself find Neo-Confucianism very difficult, too.

At first, the new ideology was espoused only by a minority ruling class and failed to gain widespread acceptance among ordinary people. It was hard for the commoners, who had believed in Buddhism throughout the Three Kingdoms and Goryeo periods, to abandon their faith in favor of Neo-Confucianism overnight.

It took a long time for the Three Bonds and Five Relationships, filial piety and other Neo-Confucian moral principles to settle into the everyday life and culture of Joseon. Only after the Japanese invasions of the 1590s, some 200 years after the founding of Joseon, did its commoners finally accept these doctrines. Until then, they held on to the Buddhist customs and habits of the Goryeo period.

Yi Hwang and Gi Daeseung exchange letters

• Gi Daeseung's letter:

"Sir,

It was a delight to be so brilliantly enlightened by you last year... I was so relieved when you acknowledged my two theories regarding the Four Beginnings and Seven Emotions."

• Yi Hwang's answer:

"After receiving your last letter, in which you opened my eyes to my mistakes, I realized that my own previous message was clumsily worded and off the mark in places. I've amended it and would like you tell me if it's right or wrong now. I am also sending a second letter, and look forward to your reply."

Yi Hwang and Gi Daeseung were renowned Neo-Confucian scholars. The two men exchanged letters annually, without fail, for thirteen years. When they first began their correspondence, Yi was the head of the Royal Confucian Academy, a position equivalent to that of president of the country's leading university today, while Gi was a young scholar who had just passed the state examination. Yi was a whole twenty-six years older than Gi.

The letters exchanged by the two scholars contain details of their family lives, the methods and content of their study, and philosophical discussions. Among the latter is a very important discourse known as the Four-Seven Debate, which makes essential reading for anybody with an interest in Neo-Confucianism. It's a bit complicated, but here's an explanation:

The Four Beginnings are attributes with which every person is born: the capacities for sympathy, for shame at one's own mistakes and resentment for those of others, for yielding, and for distinguishing between right and wrong. The Seven Emotions are happiness, anger, sadness, pleasure, love, hate and greed. The debate between Yi and Gi was aimed at determining what gives rise to the Four Beginnings and the Seven Emotions, and how they relate to each other. You might find these concepts difficult for now, but take a closer look at them if you ever become more interested in philosophy later on.

CHAPTER 7

Neo-Confucians: a new breed of literati sparks purges

The king took the leaf from her. What he saw astonished him.
"There are four characters cut into it: '走肖爲王'!"
"Don't the characters '走' and '肖' make the character '趙!' when
you put them together? That's Jo Gwangjo's surname. Forgive me
for saying this, but the rumor on the street is that Jo will become
king."
Jungjong's tightly pursed lips began to tremble.
So how on earth did these characters end up on the leaf?

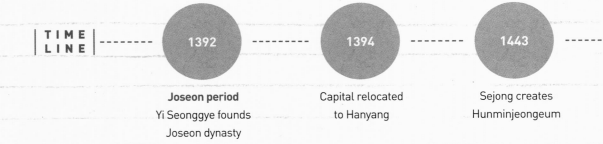

TIME LINE

1392
Joseon period
Yi Seonggye founds
Joseon dynasty

1394
Capital relocated
to Hanyang

1443
Sejong creates
Hunminjeongeum

Have you ever heard the term sahwa? *Translated literally from Sino-Korean, it means "disaster met by literati." Here, the literati in question are those belonging to the* sarim *faction, also known as the Neo-Confucian literati. At the time, officials in the royal court were divided into two factions: the* hungu, *also known as the meritorious elite, and the Neo-Confucian literati. The former were elderly meritorious subjects with abundant money and political power. The latter, meanwhile, had emerged as critics of the meritorious elite. Their ranks were largely concentrated in the Office of the Inspector-General, the Office of the Censor-General and the Office of Special Advisors. Collectively, these three offices played the role of assessing the behavior of the king and other officials, and offering them criticism and advice.*

The three offices were generally staffed by young officials at the dawns of their careers. Their criticism of the meritorious elite was ferocious as they accused them of engaging in corruption to further increase their own wealth and power.

Eventually, the two factions began a fierce power struggle. Each time this boiled over into purge of one faction at the instigation of the other, the incident was referred to as a "sahwa." In the period lasting from the reign of King Yeonsangun to that of King Myeongjong, no fewer than four sahwa *took place. So who was the eventual winner?*

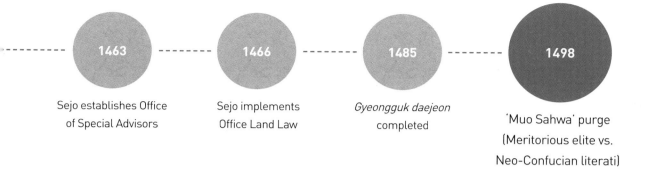

1463 — Sejo establishes Office of Special Advisors

1466 — Sejo implements Office Land Law

1485 — *Gyeongguk daejeon* completed

1498 — 'Muo Sahwa' purge (Meritorious elite vs. Neo-Confucian literati)

The meritorious elite had first emerged under King Sejo, who came to power by usurping his young nephew, Danjong. Sejo was the second son of King Sejong; before taking the throne, he was known as Prince Suyang.

Danjong became king when he was twelve years old. As he was too young to engage in politics, the state councillors at the time, including Kim Jongseo and Hwang Boin, took on his political duties. This meant, of course, that Danjong was effectively a mere figurehead. Suyang disapproved strongly of this. He therefore had Kim Jongseo and Hwang Boin killed, drove Danjong into exile, and installed himself on the throne.

Sejo appointed his supporters as meritorious subjects, giving them plenty of land and slaves as gifts. Despite already possessing large amounts of money and power, however,

Cheongnyeongpo
The dense pine wood on the other side of this river is where Danjong was sent into exile after being dethroned. Called Cheongnyeonpo, it is effectively a natural prison, with a river flowing around three sides and a sheer cliff on the fourth. Without a boat, escape is impossible. Danjong was exiled here and killed a few months later. He was seventeen years old. Visitors to Cheongnyeongpo today can see the house where he lived and the pagoda he built as he pined for his wife.

'Jo Uije mun'
This text was a lament for the Chinese Emperor Yi of Chu, who had been driven into exile by Xiang Yu. The meritorious elite interpreted it as likening Emperor Yi to the dethroned King Danjong, and Xiang Yu to his uncle and usurper, King Sejo.

they engaged without hesitation in all kinds of corruption in order to acquire even more.

The Neo-Confucian literati frequently slammed the corruption of the meritorious elite. In turn, the latter began looking for a chance to get back at the young officials snapping at their heels. In the end, the meritorious elite made the first attack, on a trifling pretext. This was the first *sahwa*. It took place during the reign of King Yeonsangun.

Neo-Confucian literati vs. meritorious elite: round one

One day, Yi Geukdon, one of the meritorious elite, showed a text to Yu Jagwang:

"Take a look at this! It's by a young man named Kim Ilson, and it brings shame on King Sejo."

Kim was a young official, just thirty-five years old, whose job was to write sacho-documents used to compile royal annals. Yi, meanwhile, was sixty-four years old and a leading member of the meritorious elite. The text by Kim that Yi showed Yu praised *Jo Uije mun* ("Lament for the Righteous Emperor"), a work by Kim Jongjik.

The latter, Kim Ilson's teacher, was held in high esteem by the Neo-Confucian literati as their founding father.

Jo Uije mun indirectly criticized King Sejo for killing his nephew, Danjong, and taking the throne for himself. This implied not only that Sejo had been wrong, but also that his successor, Seongjong, and even his successor, Yeonsangun, should never have been king.

Yi and Yu slapped their own thighs in glee. They had found a way to get rid of all the Neo-Confucian literati at a stroke.

"This is extremely serious. We must tell His Majesty immediately."

Yu ran straight to Yeonsangun. The king, who was already fed up with the way the Neo-Confucian literati stuck their noses into everything, hit the roof.

"Insulting Sejo the Great is a very serious crime. Have Kim Jongjik severely punished."

Kim had died long ago. His corpse was therefore subjected to a punishment known as *bugwanchamsi*, which involved digging it out of its tomb and "killing" it all over again. Kim

Ilson and several dozen other Neo-Confucian literati were either put to death or punished in other ways. This purge took place in 1498, a year named *muo* according to the lunar calendar. It is therefore known as the "Muo Sahwa."

Death to those who show contempt for the king

The second *sahwa* purge was due to an incident involving Lady Yun, Yeonsangun's mother. Once a royal concubine, had become Seongjong's consort and borne Yeonsangun. But her strongly jealous character had seen her suddenly expelled from the palace and condemned to death by drinking poison. Yeonsangun was just a four-year-old boy at the time and knew none of this. It was only at the age of nineteen, three months after becoming king, that he found out about his mother's deposition and death. He first caught wind of the affair when reading the epitaph that had been written for his father's tomb. That day, he refused to eat.

At the time Yeonsangun did not make a big issue of what had happened to his mother. He was not yet much of a despot. But as time passed, he grew sick of the way his ministers criticized every little thing, and started suspecting that they looked down on him.

Ten years later, in an effort to get into Yeonsangun's good books, a man by the name of Im Sahong told him the story

of how his mother had died. Lady Yun had been deposed after Eom and Jeong, two of Seongjong's concubines, slandered her, he said. Enraged, Yeonsangun had Eom and Jeong beaten to death. Not only that: he shouted at his grandmother, Queen Dowager Insu, who had reserved a particular hatred for Lady Yun, "Why did you kill my mother?" The queen dowager died not long afterwards, perhaps due to shock at her grandson's outburst.

While he was at it, Yeonsangun resolved to punish all the ministers who looked down on him. He had all those who had agreed with the dethronement of his mother, all those who had not actively opposed it, and all those he deemed generally lacking in respect for him killed. Many of these were Neo-Confucian literati. This second purge took place in the year 1504, the Joseon calendar name of which was *gapja*, and is therefore known as the Gapja Sahwa.

Yeonsangun grew progressively more vicious. In the end, he himself was deposed and succeeded by his half-brother, who became King Jungjong. This event is known as the Jungjong Restoration; among its leading proponents were members of the meritorious elite. Driven into a corner by the wild despot, they had finally taken matters into their own hands.

Did Jo Gwangjo try to become king?

After toppling Yeonsangun and putting Jungjong on the throne, the meritorious elite felt more emboldened than ever. Jungjong always had to honor their opinions, since they had helped him become king in the first place. Now, though, they found themselves challenged head-on by a man named Jo Gwangjo. Jo held the powerful position of inspector-general and enjoyed the full support of the Neo-Confucian literati.

At first, Jungjong also trusted and favored Jo. The meritorious elite, however, undermined this trust by spreading false rumors. The key protagonists among them were Hong Gyeongju, Sim Jeong and Nam Gon.

"Everyone looks up to Jo Gwangjo."

"He's so popular now that he's in government."

These rumors eventually reached the ears of the king, as intended. At the same time, Hong set in motion a plot involving his daughter, a royal concubine. She went to see the king:

"Something strange has happened. I found this leaf in the garden behind the palace. There's something etched into it."

The king took the leaf from her. What he saw astonished him:

Jo Gwangjo
Jo was a leading member of the Neo-Confucian literati faction. He believed cultivation of the heart and mind to be of central importance in study.

"There are four characters cut into it: '走肖爲王'!"

"Don't the characters '走' and '肖' make the character '趙' when you put them together? That's Jo Gwangjo's surname. Forgive me for saying this, but the rumor on the street is that Jo will become king."

Jungjong's tightly pursed lips began to tremble. So how on earth did these characters end up on the leaf? Somebody had written them first in a sweet liquid that insects love to eat. Sure enough, bugs came along and munched their way across the leaf, following the tasty liquid and etching the characters as they went. Now that the king was suddenly suspicious, Nam, Hong and Sim went to see him. Jo was plotting a conspiracy, they said. Jungjong had Jo and his followers in the Neo-Confucian literati banished or killed. Jo himself was condemned to death by drinking poison. This third purge took place in 1519, *gimyo*, and is therefore known as Gimyo Sahwa.

The '走肖爲王' incident
Jungjong is dumbfounded after seeing the characters "走肖爲王" eaten into a leaf. This was part of a plot by the meritorious elite faction aimed at getting rid of Jo Gwangjo. It resulted in his death at the age of just thirty-eight.

Final victory for the Neo-Confucian literati

The fourth and final purge occurred during the reign of Myeongjong, son of Jungjong and Queen Munjeong, his third wife. Jungjong's second wife, Queen Janggyeong, died after giving birth to a son named Injong. Injong appeared set to

Tomb of Queen Munjeong
Munjeong is buried alone at Taereung Royal Tomb, near what is today Korea National Training Center, a facility for athletes. She wanted to be buried together with her late husband, King Jungjong, but his tomb, Jeongneung (now known as Seonjeongneung and located in Samseong-dong, southern Seoul) was prone to flooding during the monsoon season and deemed a poor site.

become an outstanding monarch, and the Neo-Confucian literati pinned high hopes on him. Suddenly, though, he died after just nine months on the throne. The story goes that he fell sick after eating rice cakes fed to him by Queen Munjeong and never recovered.

Eventually, Myeongjong became king. He was only twelve years old at the time, and too young to actually perform the duties of a king. As a result, he became a mere figurehead, while his mother, Queen Munjeong, exercised royal power in his place. Munjeong effectively ruled Joseon for the next two decades.

The queen now joined forces with her younger brother, Yun Wonhyeong, to drive out Injong's maternal uncle, Yun Im. At the same time, she found various pretexts to eliminate any Neo-Confucian literati that criticized her. Many of them were killed or banished. This purge took place in the year *eulsa* (1545) and is therefore known as the Eulsa Sahwa. As long as Munjeong remained alive, the Neo-Confucians found themselves excluded from the royal court.

All four of the purges that began under Yeonsangun and ended under Myeongjong resulted in losses for the Neo-Confucian literati. But their defeat was far from total: ultimately, in fact, they emerged as the winning faction. How?

Those Neo-Confucian literati that did manage to survive

the purges retreated to the countryside, where they gradually developed power bases centered around *seowon* (Confucian academies). It was here that they educated their own students, gradually bolstering their factional strength.

Once Munjeong and Myeongjong were dead and King Seonjo on the throne, the Neo-Confucian literati made a comeback in the royal court. From then on, power was in their hands and they came to monopolize Joseon politics. Ultimately, they had won.

 'Seowon,' 'hyanggyo' and 'seodang'

Seowon, *hyanggyo* and *seodang* were all equivalents to today's schools. *Seowon* and *seodang* were private, while *hyanggyo* were run by the state. *Seowon* and *hyanggyo* also functioned as places for holding rites to great scholars such as Confucius and Yi Hwang. *Seodang* were similar to elementary schools today, while *seowon* and *hyanggyo* corresponded to middle and high schools. The sons of *yangban* families tended to study at private *seowon* rather than public *hyanggyo*, while commoners generally attended the latter. Though *seowon* were originally established to cultivate talented individuals and teach Neo-Confucianism in the provinces, they gradually became associated with various political groups and grew into hotbeds of factionalism.

Sosu Seowon
This was Korea's first *seowon*, established in 1542 by Ju Sebung while governor of Punggi in Gyeongsang-do Province. Located in the town of Yeongju, it was originally named Baegundong Seowon. This changed when King Myeongjong came up with the new name Sosu Seowon and wrote the signboard for it in his own hand. *Seowon* that received signboards from the king in this way became known as *saaek seowon*.

Seong Sammun and Sin Sukju

"I wanted to kill you. You stole our country."
Seong Sammun answered his torturers
bluntly. He addressed Sejo, who had become
king after dethroning Danjong, as "you,"
refusing to recognize him as a legitimate
monarch. Park Paengnyeon, Ha Wiji, Yi
Gae, Yu Seongwon and Yu Eungbu were also
dragged before Sejo and tortured. The king
was having their legs burned using red-hot
iron rods.

Park was as defiant as Seong. "You'd better
heat up this rod again, it's getting cold!" he
said. "Your punishments are very cruel, you
know."

Tombs of the Sayuksin
Originally, this site was home only to the tombs of Park
Paengnyeon, Seong Sammun, Yu Eungbu and Yi Gae. Later on,
empty tombs in memory of Ha Wiji, Ryu Seungwon and Kim
Mungi were added.

Park eventually died in prison, while the others were dragged
outside and executed. Collectively, they are known as the
Sayuksin, or "Six Martyred Ministers." At first, Seong recognized
Sejo's enthronement and was even proclaimed a meritorious
subject by the new king. As time went by, however, Sejo paid less
and less attention to his ministers and placed himself increasingly
at the center of government. In doing this, he was attempting to
restore the royal authority and dignity that had weakened under
King Danjong due to his young age. Seong, however, believed

it was wrong for the king to ignore his ministers and rule by himself. This is why he had hatched a plan to topple Sejo and restore Danjong to the throne.

One man was particularly churned up as he silently watched Seong being tortured: his friend, Sin Sukju. The two men had worked together in Jiphyeonjeon since the time of King Sejong. Sin, however, had not been a part of Seong's plot. This was because he believed Sejo was right in trying to increase the authority of the king. In his view, the country could not function properly as long as the monarch remained weak.

Later on, Seong was praised as a loyal subject, while Sin was condemned as a turncoat to the extent where mung bean sprouts are called "Sukju sprouts" in Korean because they are the quickest to turn sour. In fact, though, they had merely chosen divergent paths because of their different beliefs. Can we really say for sure which one of them was right?

Portrait of Sin Sukju
Sin and Seong Sammun played active roles in the creation and diffusion of Hunminjeongeum. Sejong valued both men highly. Sin was one year older than Seong, but the two were very close as friends and colleagues. Once Sejo came to the throne, however, their lives took very different paths.

CHAPTER 8

Clothes, food and housing in Joseon

Does that mean people in Joseon ate no lunch whatsoever? In summer, when the days were long, they ate three meals a day, including a simple lunch. In winter, when each day was shorter, they ate only two. For a king, however, it was not uncommon to eat five meals a day: breakfast, lunch and dinner, plus an early-morning bite and a late-night snack.

TIME LINE

1546
Regular markets open
in several provinces

1554
Eo Sukgwon writes
Gosa chwaryo

1559
Im Kkeokjeong's rebellion
in Hwanghae-do Province

Have you ever heard of the "nation dressed in white?"

Such was the fondness of Koreans for white clothing that this became one of their nicknames. It seems to make some people think that Koreans wore white clothes from time immemorial all the way to the end of the Joseon period.

In fact, Koreans enjoyed wearing a variety of colorful clothing throughout the Three Kingdoms period, Goryeo and even into Joseon. In the latter, they wore blue, pink and plenty more. Men preferred lighter shades, while women and children enjoyed bright, vivid colors. It's completely wrong to assume that the people of Joseon wore nothing but white.

Since we're on the subject, I'd like to tell you today about the clothes the people of Joseon wore, the food they ate and the homes they lived in. This should give you some idea of how different things were back then.

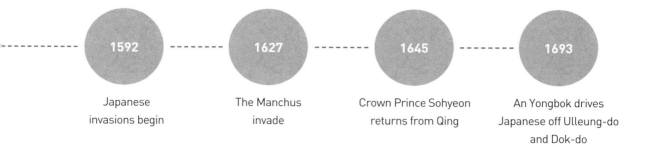

1592	1627	1645	1693
Japanese invasions begin	The Manchus invade	Crown Prince Sohyeon returns from Qing	An Yongbok drives Japanese off Ulleung-do and Dok-do

Have you ever seen a painting called *Miindo*? Its subject is a beautiful woman, dressed and coiffed immaculately and showing just a tantalizing trace of a smile. Her abundant, long hair, short, tight jacket and ballooning, pleated skirt cut a lovely figure. This painting gives us a good idea of how women dressed in Joseon.

Joseon and the appearance of 'jeogori'

It was in the Joseon period that Koreans began wearing jackets known as *jeogori*. So what did they wear before?

Before the advent of the *jeogori*, people wore upper garments called *yu*. These came down to cover part of their buttocks, like taekwondo uniforms, and were fastened at

'Miindo'
Elaborately plaited hair, a billowing skirt and a tight jacket—this painting, an heirloom of the Yun family of Haenam, offers a snapshot of women's fashion in Joseon period. –Nogudang

Commoner women's clothing
Skirts in Joseon differed according to social class. Those of *yangban* women were long and wide; those of commoners shorter and narrower. They had to be, if the women who wore them were to work with any degree of comfort.
–National Museum of Korea

the waist by a belt. *Yu* were worn by both men and women throughout the Three Kingdoms and Goryeo periods. The *jeogori* differed from the *yu* in that it was shorter, reaching down only to a point above the waist, and was therefore fastened with a coat string instead of a belt.

At first, the *jeogori* worn by men and women looked almost the same. As time passed, however, the version worn by women grew shorter, eventually reaching the point where it covered little more than the armpits. Short *jeogori* were originally fashionable among *gisaeng*, but this trend gradually spread to women in *yangban* families and, eventually, to commoners too.

Yangban women wore long, extremely wide skirts. Most luxurious were those known as *seuranchima*, which were hemmed with fabric containing gold thread. Commoner women wore shorter, narrower skirts that came roughly down to their shins and were easy to wear when working. Such skirts were known as *mongdangchima*.

Whenever *yangban* women went out in public, they had to wear garments known as *jangot*, *sseugaechima* or *neoul* to cover their faces. It wasn't considered respectable for an aristocratic woman to walk around with her face on display for everyone to see. A *jangot* was similar to the overcoat commonly worn by men, called a *durumagi*, while a *sseugaechima* resembled a normal skirt in shape but was slightly smaller. A *neoul,*

● 'Yangban' dressed for an outing

– National Museum of Korea

| A man's clothes |
– National Folk Museum of Korea

'gat' (horsehair hat)

'sultti' (tasseled belt)

'dopo' (robe)

'haengjeon' (puttees)

'baji' (pants)

'nokpihye' (deerskin shoes)

| A woman's clothes | – National Folk Museum of Korea

'jangot' (robe)

'sseugaechima' (shawl)

'jeogori' (jacket)

'chima' (skirt)

'norigae' (ornament)

'beoseon' (socks)

'unhye' (cloud-patterned shoes)

meanwhile, was made of fabric thin enough to see through, which covered the face and extended down to shoulder height.

Commoner women had no need to cover their faces when they went out. How could farmers' wives or female slaves have worn anything as impractical as a *jangot* or a *sseugaechima* as they worked anyway?

'Gache' and 'gat:' the bigger, the better

Women's most striking attempts at beautification came in the form of their hairstyles. Take another look at the woman in the painting, *Miindo*, and the way her hair has been braided into thick plaits and arranged in coils on top of her head. This was called a *gache*. In fact, it was a kind of wig. After combing her hair and putting it up, a woman would place the *gache* on top of it.

Gache were very expensive, so that only well-off homes could afford them. Still, in those days, just as now, nobody was indifferent to fashion. Every woman wanted a *gache*. The bigger it was, the closer its owner to the very cutting edge of fashion.

As well as being expensive, *gache* were very heavy. There's even one story - which we shouldn't laugh at - of a thirteen-year-old bride standing up suddenly when her father-in-

'Gache singeum samok'
This law, promulgated in 1788 during the reign of King Jeongjo, banned women from wearing *gache*. While the original text was written in classical Chinese, a Hangeul version was included to make it easy for women to understand.
– Kyujanggak Institute for Korean Studies

law entered the room and having her neck broken by the sheer weight of her *gache*. In certain other cases, women were unable to get married because they couldn't afford to buy a *gache*. With all the trouble they caused, these wigs eventually became the object of an official ban by the

–National Museum of Korea

Women wearing 'gache'

government. Women were instructed to wear much lighter headpieces, called *jokduri*, instead. Still, the *gache* wasn't about to disappear that easily.

What about men? A woman's class could be distinguished according to the skirt she wore, while men's status was indicated by different versions of a cape-like garment known as a *po*. The *po* was worn over a man's jacket and trousers; different types included the *dopo*, the *changot* and the *durumagi*.

Stylish Joseon literati

Dopo and *changot* were worn by men of *yangban* status, while *durumagi* were worn by commoners. The latter weren't allowed to wear *dopo* or *changot*. Toward the end of the Joseon period, however, *yangban* and commoners alike wore *durumagi*. Indeed, even men today wear a *durumagi* as their overgarment when dressing in *hanbok*.

A man's greatest expression of style came through his

gat, a kind of hat made from horsehair and bamboo. As with the *gache*, bigger meant more fashionable. In Joseon, the most stylish man imaginable would have worn a broad, ample ramie *dopo,* a *sultti* wound from colored thread and loosely fastened at his waist, and an enormous *gat.*

Don't talk while you're eating!

Let's have a look at how people ate in Joseon.

When I was young, adults always used to tell children not to talk at mealtimes. Rather than sitting round the dinner table and chatting away about what they had done that day, etiquette dictated that families should sit and eat in silence.

Why was this? Because of the influence of Confucianism and Buddhism. Confucius is said never to have spoken while eating, or while in bed. During meals, he concentrated solely on eating; after going to bed, he focused entirely on sleeping. These habits of the great sage were held up as exemplary behavior throughout the Joseon period, a tradition that survived even when I was a child. According to Buddhist tradition, too, monks never speak while eating during practice. They remain silent in order to concentrate fully on every taste and feeling. These days, in complete contrast

Lunch
These men have gathered to eat lunch and are sharing out food brought to them on women's heads, and drinks delivered on an A-frame. After a hard morning's work, lunch tasted sublime.
–National Folk Museum of Korea

to the Joseon period, exchanging friendly conversation at mealtimes is considered a happier experience. Though speaking with a mouth full of food is still a bit much.

Did people in Joseon eat three meals a day, like us? No. Most of them ate only two: breakfast and dinner. Im Gwon, an official during the reign of King Myeongjong, told the king that "A person must eat two meals a day" in order not to starve, but that there had been a poor harvest that year and the people were not even getting one meal a day, and therefore needed to be saved by the state.

Does that mean people in Joseon ate no lunch whatsoever? In summer, when the days were long, they ate three meals a day, including a simple lunch. In winter, when each day was shorter, they ate only two.

For a king, however, it was not uncommon to eat five meals a day: breakfast, lunch and dinner, plus an early-morning bite and a late-night snack. The two extra meals were not of rice but of things like *juk* (rice porridge), noodles, rice cakes, tea and lighter snacks. When the king did eat a proper rice-based meal, it was one of abundance. After he had had his fill, court ladies would gather to share the leftovers.

Not all kings ate five times a day, though: each monarch had his own personal dining habits. Yeongjo, for example, had poor digestion and preferred not to eat a lot. He took just four meals a day, skipping the first breakfast; from the

The origins of 'jeomsim'
The Sino-Korean word for lunch, *jeomsim*, is a combination of the characters "點" (an ink dot) and "心" (heart and mind). Originating from Tang China, this word refers to a simple snack that is just sufficient to bring a bit of life back to a body and mind flagging with hunger. In China, the word is still used to describe a snack rather than a full meal.

age of thirty-five, he further reduced this diet to just two daily meals. Jeongjo, too, ate only twice a day, choosing simple meals of just three or four *banchan* (side dishes) on a single plate. When did Koreans start eating three meals a day, then? Surprisingly, only in the twentieth century.

One unique Korean dining habit is the use of a spoon. Several other countries, including Japan, China and Vietnam, use chopsticks too, but Korea is the only one to combine them with a spoon. Originally, Japan and China also used spoons, but this practice grew less and less frequent until only chopsticks remained.

 The origins of sweet potatoes and potatoes

The potatoes and sweet potatoes that Koreans enjoy as snacks these days were first brought into the country two or three hundred years ago. Before then, nobody had an inkling of their existence.

Sweet potatoes were first imported in the mid-eighteenth century by Jo Eom, a Joseon envoy returning from a visit to the Japanese island of Tsushima. The locals on Tsushima called the tubers *kokkoimo*, a word that ended up pronounced in Korean as *goguma*. Another Korean word sometimes used for the sweet potato is *gamjeo*.

Potatoes arrived later, in the early nineteenth century. They are said to have been dropped by somebody from Qing who had sneaked over the border into Joseon to look for ginseng. At first, they were called *bukgamjeo*, meaning "sweet potatoes from the north," or *maryeongseo*, meaning "horse bell yam," because of the way they hung in clusters like round horse bells when pulled from the earth.

Sweet potatoes and potatoes occasionally kept poor commoners from starving to death in lean years, thanks to the way they stayed alive and kept growing even in times of drought.

When Sin Sukju traveled to Japan as an envoy during the reign of King Sejong, he was amazed to see the Japanese eating only with chopsticks. Perhaps the reason Koreans have held onto the spoon is because they eat some kind of soup, broth or other liquid dish as part

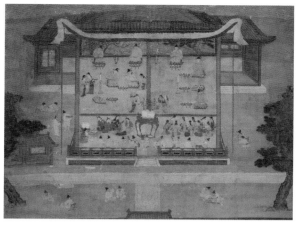

'Giyeonghoedo'
This painting shows elderly retired officials gathering for a party. Take a good look: each guest has been served a meal on his own individual table.

of most meals. If you're eating soups and stews with bits and pieces of food in them, you can't get by without a spoon.

At first, people all over the world ate using only their hands. Even in the West, where so much emphasis is placed on table manners, they started off with nothing but bare hands. Judging by the fact that sixteenth-century French philosopher Michel de Montaigne claimed to have bitten his own fingers while eating too fast, it appears that people still used their hands to put food straight into their mouths even at this time. This is why Westerners developed the custom of washing their hands before eating.

While families today sit around a single dining table to eat, in the Joseon period each person had his own. This custom was maintained even at parties. Mind you, it only applied to male members of *yangban* households, not to commoners or women. The latter would often just gulp down a quick meal in the kitchen, or eat from dishes placed straight on the floor instead of on a table. That's a bit much, you might say. Well, sexual and class-based discrimination extended to mealtimes just as it did to almost every other area.

My ideal home

During the reign of King Sukjong some 330 years ago, seventy-two-year-old official Yi Yutae was living in exile in Yeongbyeon, Pyeongan-do Province. Worn down by this hard life, he wrote a text fantasizing about his ideal home.

"First, I'll build a five-*kan* house with a tiled roof [a *kan*, the space between two columns, was used in Joseon as a unit for measuring building area]. I'll give one *kan* to my children, use one as a *maru* [unheated, wooden-floored area] to store my belongings, two as bedrooms, and the last one as a kitchen. When my children grow up, the house will be too small. I'll have an annex built for me and my three sons and I'll add another three-*kan* building with one *kan* as the *bang* [room with a heated *ondol* floor], one as a *maru* and one as a kitchen. Then my son or daughter can move in with his wife or her husband later on... For the men's quarters, a three-*kan* building will suffice; two *kan* as *bang* and one as a *maru*. I'll put doors between the *bang* and the *dang* [the main *maru* space], and use the latter for holding ancestral rites... I'll need a stable next

'Yangban' home
This is the former house of Kim Jeonghui, the Joseon scholar and calligrapher famous for creating the style of script known as Chusache. The house is called Chusa Gotaek (Chusa was Kim's pen name). Those entering through the front gate first come to the *sarangchae* (above); further in lies the *anchae* (below). The former was used by the master of the household for reading and receiving guests, while the latter was inhabited by the mistress of the household, who was in charge of its day-to-day running.

to the men's annex, preferably where it can be seen when the northern window is open… And it would be good to have a study next to the men's quarters *Sarangchae*, too, where children can read books. I'll stop any idle people coming in, and bar even relatives and neighbors'

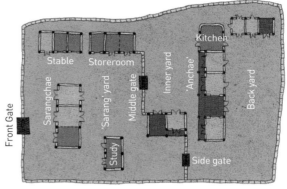

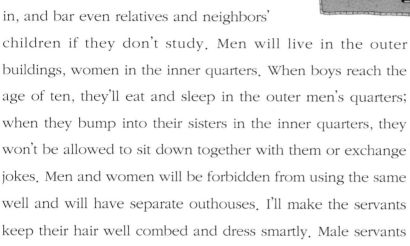

Yi Yutae's dream house
This drawing is based on Yi Yutae's description of his dream house.
(Sin Yeonghun, 'Hanguk-ui sallimjip' ('Korean Homes'))

children if they don't study. Men will live in the outer buildings, women in the inner quarters. When boys reach the age of ten, they'll eat and sleep in the outer men's quarters; when they bump into their sisters in the inner quarters, they won't be allowed to sit down together with them or exchange jokes. Men and women will be forbidden from using the same well and will have separate outhouses. I'll make the servants keep their hair well combed and dress smartly. Male servants won't be allowed in the inner quarters except to sweep the courtyard. And definitely not in the kitchen…"

What do you think of that? Can you picture Yu's dream house for yourself? His fantasy describes the ideal home of a Joseon *yangban*. Keeping men and women, masters and *nobi* in strictly delimited living spaces, in particular, was an embodiment of Neo-Confucian ideals.

Indeed, Joseon *yangban* did build and live in houses like the one of which Yu dreamt. If you visit one of those that still stand today, you'll see the clearly divided outer men's quarters,

Thatched houses
This image shows a village of thatched houses, interspersed by narrow streets. In Joseon, each village only had one or two tiled *yangban* houses; the rest had thatched roofs and were inhabited by commoners. The scene here is an excerpt from a painting called *Jeonju jido*.

inner women's quarters and separate servant's quarters.

What about commoners, then? *Chogasamgan* is a phrase in Korean that literally means "three *kan* and a grass roof" and is used to describe an extremely humble abode with just a couple of small rooms and a kitchen under a thatched roof. Houses like these had no imposing front gates or perimeter walls like those of *yangban*, just a fence of sorts and a permanently open space for a gate. With just one or two rooms in total, maintaining separate spaces for men and women in the style of a *yangban* household was out of the question.

Children's games

These days, most children, boys and girls alike, love computer games. But how did children keep themselves amused back in the simpler days of Joseon?

Joseon children knew plenty of fun games. Have you ever heard the Korean term *jungmagou*? Literally meaning "bamboo horse old friend," it means a close childhood friend whom you've known since the days you played together on bamboo horses. Bamboo horse riding is a traditional game in which each player cuts two bamboo stems of her or his own height, finds or makes footholds on each one, then rides them like stilts. Players race to a fixed point and back, while singing a special song.

One other game, which children still play today, is hide-and-seek. In Korean, it's called *sullaejapgi*, a word derived from *sulla*, the equivalent of a patrolling policeman in the Joseon period.

Joseon children played plenty of other games in addition to these: boys spent their time spinning tops, flying kites, tossing stones, kicking shuttlecock-like toys called *jegi*, and hitting sticks; girls played at marbles, making straw dolls, see-saw jumping, circle-dancing, and whizzing through the air on rope swings. Games like *yut* and tug-of-war were enjoyed by boys and girls alike.

See-saw jumping
Girls enjoyed playing on see-saws within the compounds of their own homes. This picture is by late-Joseon painter Kim Jungeun.

Kicking a 'jegi'

CHAPTER 9

Newspapers
and books in Joseon

These days, books are simply products that anybody can buy from a bookshop. And they're much cheaper than they were in Joseon. While information and knowledge were once the preserve of a small minority of individuals, they are now read by huge numbers of ordinary people. The Internet, meanwhile, has thrown open the door to a veritable treasure trove of knowledge for anyone interested in entering.

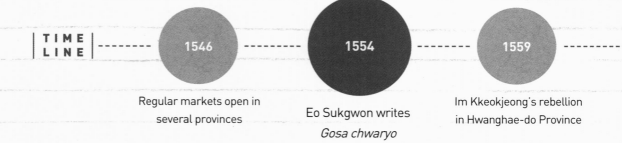

TIME LINE - - - - - - - - 1546 - - - - - - - - 1554 - - - - - - - - 1559 - - - - - - - - -

1546 Regular markets open in several provinces

1554 Eo Sukgwon writes *Gosa chwaryo*

1559 Im Kkeokjeong's rebellion in Hwanghae-do Province

Did they have newspapers in the old days, too? Of course: there was an official bulletin, called the Jobo. And, needless to say, plenty of books and bookshops.

Korea today is sometimes described as an "information-based society," reflecting the importance of information in our lives. We have many novel ways of transmitting and receiving it—television, newspaper, magazines, the Internet, books and so on—but recognition of its importance is nothing new. The people of Joseon, too, were well aware of the value of information. So how did they convey it? There was no television or Internet, of course, but there was the Jobo. This newspaper, however, was only available to a small minority of officials and other members of the ruling class.

This newspaper, however, was only available to a small minority of officials and other members of the ruling class. The same went for books, too.

Today, let's take a look at the kind of newspapers and books available to the citizens of Joseon.

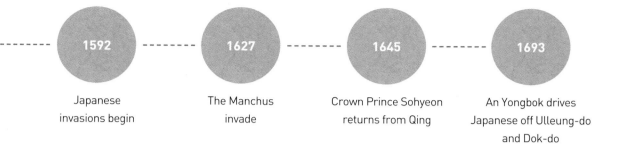

1592	1627	1645	1693
Japanese invasions begin	The Manchus invade	Crown Prince Sohyeon returns from Qing	An Yongbok drives Japanese off Ulleung-do and Dok-do

Today, a variety of newspapers is published. These include dailies, evening papers, weeklies and even papers especially for young children. In the Joseon period, however, there was only one newspaper, published every morning: the Jobo. While most newspapers today are published privately, the *Jobo* was produced by the state; its title literally means "news from the royal court." The *Jobo* was also sometimes known as the *Jeobo*, the *Gibyeol* or the *Gibyeolji*.

The *Jobo* was compiled by the Royal Secretariat, an office similar to today's Presidential Secretariat. This department dealt with all royal commands and

'Chaekgado'
Still life works showing piles of books, brush holders, brushes and other items like these were known as *chaekgado* or *munbangdo*. They look ideal for hanging in a study, and that's generally where they were found, encouraging their owners to study hard.
–National Folk Museum of Korea

passed on all reports and appeals submitted to the king. Effectively, all important information and news in the nation flowed through it.

Hand-copied news

Newspapers today are produced by a process in which journalists cover news stories and write articles, which are then compiled into a newspaper layout by editors and printed on a rotary press. Printed newspapers are distributed to each area and delivered to the houses of subscribers.

The process of producing the *Jobo* was very different, in that each edition was not printed by machine but copied by hand.

Articles were collected by the Royal Secretariat every morning, based on various bits of information it received. After officials decided what to include and what to omit, the office compiled the selected articles into a newspaper and published them. This happened in a place known as the Joboso or the Gibyeolcheong. It was here that scribes from each government office waited early in the morning for news items to be announced. They wrote down each article by hand as it was announced, in Chinese characters, using a special, flowing style that allowed them to record the information rapidly. This style of handwriting was known as

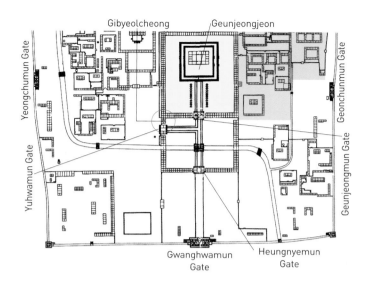

Gibyeolcheong   Geunjeongjeon

Yeongchumun Gate

Yuhwamun Gate

Geonchunmun Gate

Geunjeongmun Gate

Gwanghwamun Gate   Heungnyemun Gate

Gibyeolcheong, Gyeongbokgung Palace
The *Jobo* was published by the Gibyeolcheong. The map of Gyeongbokgung Palace on the left shows how those entering Heungnyemun Gate would then see another gate, Yuhwamun, on the left. Yuhwamun led to an area in which several government offices and departments were located. The Gibyeolcheong was situated just next to Yuhwamun; the photo on the right shows a restored version of it.

gibyeolche and was difficult to read for anyone who had not studied Chinese characters to a considerable extent. It was an early equivalent to today's shorthand.

Once they had taken down the news in the *Jobo*, the scribes headed back to their own government offices. There, they made more handwritten copies of the bulletin, which were delivered to all those who required one. Those who delivered the *Jobo* were known as *gibyeol gunsa*. The designated recipient was indicated on the back of each copy, not by name but by neighborhood of residence or official title. Recipients of the *Jobo* in Hanyang, the Joseon capital (today's Seoul) were sent a copy every day, while those in the provinces received several accumulated editions at a time. Just as today, subscribers had to pay a fee. High-ranking officials paid four

The royal newspaper
The king also received a copy of the *Jobo*. His, though, was not written in flowing *gibyeolche* script but in neat, full Chinese characters. One official had the job of writing out this exclusive personal copy of the *Jobo* for the king.

Officials writing copies of the 'Jobo'
These officials, known as *gibyeol seori*, could be equated to the stenographers that work in parliament today.

nyang a month, while their lower-ranking counterparts paid around one *nyang* and five *jeon*.

The *Jobo* was written by hand rather than printed, despite Joseon's advanced printing technology, in order to keep the information in it confined to a small number of people. Printing would have allowed production of far more copies, giving more people access to the content. Most of the Jobo's readers at the time were officials and *yangban*, who numbered no more than a few hundred nationwide. Though this minority of individuals felt the need to share information among themselves, they did not want it leaked to others.

One illustrative example of this occurred in 1577, during the reign of King Seonjo, when several people were severely punished after mass-producing and selling printed copies of the *Jobo*. These were highly popular, since printing made them much easier to read than handwritten copies and anyone who had the money could buy one. The printed *Jobo* sold like hot cakes. When rumors of this reached the king, however, he was furious, claiming that the content of the *Jobo* would reveal Korea's domestic mistakes if it reached the outside world. Those responsible for printing and selling the paper were arrested by the State Tribunal, lashed with a sharpened cane and sent into exile. From then on, printing of the *Jobo* was completely banned.

What kind of articles made it into the 'Jobo?'

The *Jobo* contained articles about unusual natural phenomena, with headlines like "Comet appears," "Spot found on the moon," "Chick born with four feet and four wings," "Egg-sized hailstones kill birds; people die of fright." Some articles contained interpretations of natural phenomena like these, believing them to be a reflection of disorder created by poor government. Rainfall and the first frost of the year were recorded without fail, due to their importance for agriculture.

Supyogyo Bridge
Knowing how much rain had fallen was highly important in Joseon. Supyogyo is a bridge that measured how high the water had risen in Cheonggyecheon Stream, central Seoul. On its columns are markings that indicated the amount of precipitation. It has now been relocated to Jangchungdan Park, near Mt. Namsan.

The 'Gwanbo'

The *Gwanbo* came into print after the abolition of the *Jobo* and is similar to its predecessor in that it is published by the state. The *Gwanbo* is still published today: the photo on the left shows the first edition, published on June 21 by the lunar calendar in 1894; the photo on the right is of a recent copy.

–Ministry of Security and Public Administration

After invented the rain gauge, one was set up in the yard of every government office in the country. The head of each county had to personally check the rain gauge and report his local rainfall to Hanyang. These measurements were gathered and published in the *Jobo*.

The *Jobo* also contained news of royal orders, promotions and dismissals of officials, holidays, deaths, petitions and proposals submitted to the king, and various reports.

In cases where news was so urgent that it couldn't wait for the next day's *Jobo*, a special edition would be published immediately. This was known as a *bunbal*. When Seonjo's wife, Queen Inmok, gave birth to a daughter, the news was delivered right away in a *bunbal*.

It was forbidden, however, for certain types of news to be included in the *Jobo*. Sometimes kings would give special orders that information related to national security or sensitive diplomatic issues regarding China be omitted. Of course, the *Jobo* also functioned as an important source of reference when compiling history books such as royal annals.

After being published every day, without fail, throughout several centuries of Joseon history, the *Jobo* was discontinued as part of the Gabo Reform of 1894. Though it wasn't entirely the same as the newspapers we read today, the *Jobo* was a wonderful precursor.

Books: available only to officials and 'yangban'

Like the *Jobo*, books in Joseon were comprehensible only to the small ruling elite who could read Chinese characters. Kings regarded publishing books and having people read them as a way of publicizing the state's policies. A special government department, the Office of Editorial Review, was created and charged with publishing books.

This office published texts on the orders of the king, sometimes distributing them free of charge to officials and sometimes selling them. Effectively, it was a publishing house, printer's and bookstore, rolled into one and run by the state.

Books sold by the Office of Editorial Review were expensive, putting them out of reach of all but government officials and *yangban*. In many cases, only a small number of copies of a given book were printed, so that even those with money were often unable to buy them. The books distributed for free by the Office of Editorial Review, meanwhile, went only to officials and *yangban* and had nothing to do with ordinary commoners.

'Gosa chwaryo'
Written by scholar Eo Sukgwon, this book was a collection of information indispensable for any Joseon official. It was similar to the "common sense encyclopedias" you find in Korea today. *Gosa chwaryo* was first published in 1554 during the reign of King Jungjong. It later went into more than ten new editions.

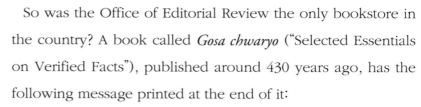

So was the Office of Editorial Review the only bookstore in the country? A book called *Gosa chwaryo* ("Selected Essentials on Verified Facts"), published around 430 years ago, has the following message printed at the end of it:

"July 1576, below Supyogyo Bridge, north side, Ha Hansu's place. Come if you want to buy."

This ambiguous message, which could equally be an advertisement or a notice, means "Copies of *Gosa chwaryo* will be printed and sold in July 1576 at Ha Hansu's house, on the northern bank [of Cheonggyecheon Stream] downstream from Supyogyo Bridge, so come along if you want one." Ha's home appears to have also been a combined publishing house, printing works and bookstore, but owned by a private citizen rather than by the state.

Metal Hangeul type and storage cabinet
Joseon metal type was extremely beautiful and accurately cast, making it a convenience and a pleasure to read printed books at the time. Type was stored in a cabinet like this one, with separate compartments for each letter.
– National Museum of Korea

It was only from around the seventeenth century, when books became much cheaper, that ordinary commoners were able to buy them. What kind of books did people buy? Textbooks such as *Thousand Character Classic* and novels such as *Guunmong* ("Cloud Dream of the Nine") and *Sa-ssi namjeong gi* ("Record of Lady Sa's Journey to the South").

These days, books are simply products that anybody can buy from a bookshop. And they're much cheaper than they were in Joseon. While information and knowledge were once

How much did books cost in Joseon?

In Joseon, books were bought in exchange for fabric or rice. The following list of prices appears in the 1576 book *Gosa chwaryo* (the *pil* was a unit used to measure rolled fabric, while the *mal* was used to measure volume, and was equivalent to ten *doe*):

Analects - 1.5 *pil* of cotton cloth, two *mal* of rice
Mencius - 1.5 *pil* of cotton cloth, two *mal* of rice
Great Learning - 1 *mal* of rice
Doctrine of the Mean - 1.5 *mal* of rice
Samgang haengsildo - 0.5 *pil* of cotton cloth, 2.5 *mal* of rice
Guwen zhenbao ("True Treasures of Ancient Literature") - 0.5 *pil* of cotton cloth, five *mal* of rice
Xiaoxue jicheng ("A Compilation of Elementary Learning") - 0.5 *pil* of cotton cloth, 1.5 *mal* of rice

One *pil* of cotton is said to have been worth about 40,000 won (about 40 US dollars) in today's money, so you can see that books weren't cheap in those days. They certainly weren't affordable to everyone; for ordinary commoners, buying them was out of the question.

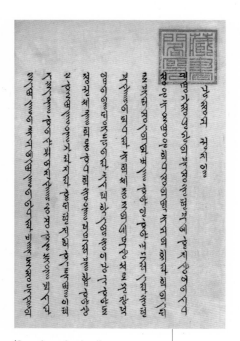

'Sa-ssi namjeong gi'
This novel was written in Hangeul, by Kim Manjung, during the reign of King Sukjong. Modeled on the story of Queen Inhyeon and Lady Jang, a royal concubine who replaced Inhyeon as queen, it became a bestseller in its time.
– National Museum of Korea

the preserve of a small minority of individuals, they are now read by huge numbers of ordinary people. The Internet, meanwhile, has thrown open the door to a veritable treasure trove of knowledge for anyone interested in entering. Ours is a world in which information can no longer be monopolized by any minority. This change is known as the "information revolution."

Royal annals: definitive national histories

Taejong Yi Bangwon was out hunting for the first time in ages. Spotting a deer, he spurred on his horse in pursuit, drawing his bowstring tight in preparation for the perfect shot. Suddenly, his horse stumbled and fell flat on its face. Taejong was flung off and sent tumbling across the ground. His pride wounded, the king turned to his ministers:

"Don't tell the court historian about this."

In the end, though, both the king's fall and his instruction not to tell the court historian made it into the official record. This should give you some idea of how meticulous the court historians of Joseon were when it came to recording every last royal word and action.

Records made by court historians of everyday events were known as *sacho*. Not even the king was allowed to read them at will. One day, Taejo Yi Seonggye asked his ministers:

"Why is it that the king can't see the historical records?"

"History must be written according to the facts and with no deliberate omissions. If the king reads the records, there's a risk that he might want to bury or overlook certain facts," they replied.

In other words, the system existed to enable historians to make proper criticisms with no qualms.

Sacho provided source material for the compilation of royal annals, chronological accounts of all the major events in the reign of a monarch that were compiled once his successor was on the throne. The *Annals of King Taejong* were compiled during the reign of Sejong, who succeeded him, while Sejong's were in turn compiled under his successor, Munjong, and so on. The royal annals are a tremendously valuable historical resource, providing information on the politics, economics, society, culture and other aspects of Joseon. They record all the major events that occurred over a period of 472 years, from the reign of Taejo to that of Cheoljong. What about Cheoljong's successors, Gojong and Sunjong? Annals of their reigns were compiled, but under the supervision of the Japanese during the colonial period. They therefore contain fabrications and omissions. When we talk about the royal annals, then, we generally mean only those up to and including the reign of Cheoljong.

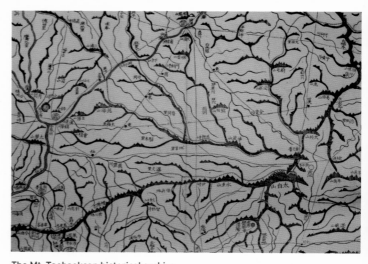

The Mt. Taebaeksan historical archive
Completed annals were sent to historical archives for safe keeping. These facilities were located deep in mountainous areas to prevent them from being burned down during wars or by accident. There were historical archives at Mt. Taebaeksan and Mt. Odaesan in Gangwon-do Province, at Mt. Jeongjoksan on Ganghwa-do Island, and at Mt. Jeoksangsan in Jeollabuk-do Province. This photo shows the archive at Mt. Taebaeksan as marked on the nineteenth-century map, *Daedong yeojido* ("Detailed Map of Korea")

Why were royal annals compiled? History is considered highly important by Confucian ideology. Confucians often find models in the words and deeds of ancestors, while seeking to leave records of their own lives for the reference of their descendants. This is why so much time and effort was devoted to the creation of the annals.

• Process of compiling the royal annals

1. Court historians record the conversations of the king and his ministers in documents called *sacho*.

2. When the king dies, the Office for Annals Compilation collects *sacho* kept by court historians, records from each government department, back issues of the *Jobo*, personal diaries and other materials. Based on these, the office produces a draft version of the annals, known as a *chocho*.

3. A revised version of the annals is made by reading through the *chocho* while taking out or amending certain content. This intermediate draft is called a *jungcho*. The *jungcho* is then edited once again to produce a final version called a *jeongcho*. Finally, the *jeongcho* is printed in the form of a series of books called annals.

4. The *sacho* and other materials used in the compilation of the annals are now put through a process called *secho*. This involves deleting everything written on the paper by rinsing it with water, and was done both in order to reuse the paper, a valuable commodity at the time, and to keep secret the information it had previously contained. *Secho* took place in the stream that flows past Segeomjeong Pavilion in today's northern Seoul, outside the old city wall.

CHAPTER 10

The Three Great Bandits of Joseon

Hong Gildong, Im Kkeokjeong and Jang Gilsan all had one thing in common: officials at the royal court branded them heinous bandits, while commoners considered them to be righteous thieves. But why would anybody have thought such men righteous?

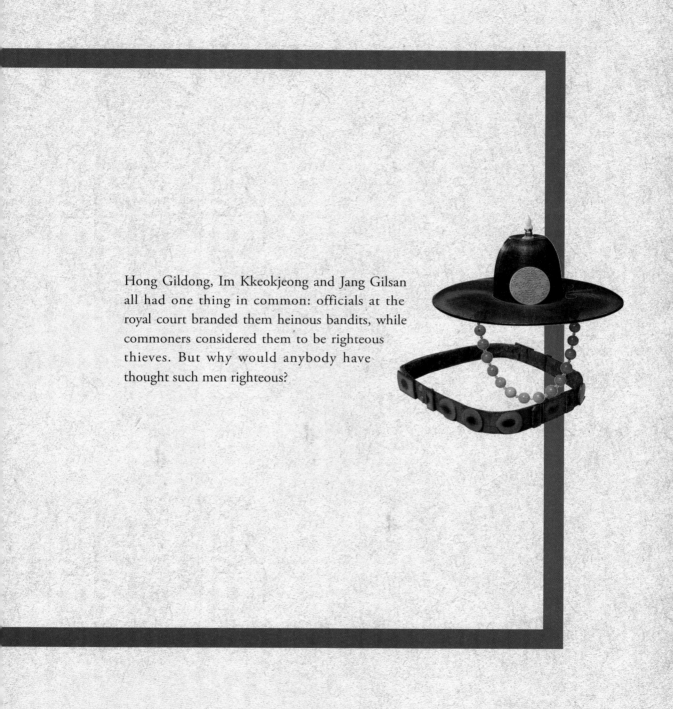

TIME LINE

1546 Regular markets open in several provinces

1554 Eo Sukgwon writes *Gosa chwaryo*

1559 Im Kkeokjeong's rebellion in Hwanghae-do Province

Have you ever read any of the novels starring Arsène Lupin, the "gentleman thief?" Lupin steals, but not from the poor or the vulnerable. On the contrary: he often helps the latter while stealing from the rich. Such characters are known in Korean as uijeok, *meaning "righteous thieves." You may have heard of Hong Gildong, one of Korea's most famous righteous thieves. Many people believe him to be a fictional character. In fact, though, he really existed and was active in Joseon some 500 years ago. Two other famous Joseon bandits were Im Kkeokjeong and Jang Gilsan. Together with Hong, they are often referred to as the Three Great Bandits of Joseon. Let's have a look at how they began their criminal careers, and how they became famous enough to be labelled righteous thieves.*

1592
Japanese
invasions begin

1627
The Manchus
invade

1645
Crown Prince Sohyeon
returns from Qing

1693
An Yongbok drives
Japanese off Ulleung-do
and Dok-do

Hong Gildong was a real thorn in the side of court officials during the reign of King Yeonsangun. He was active mainly in a region encompassing Chungcheong-do and Gyeonggi-do provinces and Seoul itself. In October, 1500, Hong was caught. Upon hearing the news of his arrest, the three state councillors, Han Chihyeong, Seong Jun and Yi Geukgyun, went to tell the king:

"We are delighted to inform you that the thief Hong Gildong has been caught. He's been going around dressed like a Security

'Okjeongja' and 'hongdae'
These accessories could only be worn by high-ranking officials. The former was made of jade and worn at the crown of a hat, while the latter was a red belt. Hong Gildong wore items such as these while impersonating officials.

–National Folk Museum of Korea

Council official, leading armed bands of followers in broad daylight and doing as he pleases."

Thieves in officials' clothing

Hong Gildong's name and actions appear more than ten times in the royal annals of Joseon, a clear indication of his significance — for better or worse.

Hong used to dress up in the garb of high-ranking officials such as *dangsanggwan* or Security Council bigwigs, walking straight into provincial government offices in broad daylight. His band of followers was so powerful that no rural leader proved capable of dealing with it.

After Hong's arrest, he was held not by the Bureau of Police, which handled common thieves, but by the State Tribunal, which dealt with *yangban* criminals and traitors: another sign of his importance in the view of the royal court.

No record, however, remains of Hong's demise. We have no way of knowing whether he died or lived, or how he was punished. There's even a rumor that he survived, traveled to the faraway Ryukyu Islands and became king there. In any case, the royal annals of Joseon only mention Hong up to the point where he is arrested, during the reign of Yeonsangun, and held by the State Tribunal.

Around 100 years after the life of the real Hong Gildong, a

novel titled *The Tale of Hong Gildong* appeared. Based on the story of the real bandit, it is widely believed to have been written by a man named Heo Gyun. Its protagonist forms the image most people have of Hong Gildong today; even now, he is remembered as the greatest righteous thief in history.

Im Kkeokjeong, the bandit of Mt. Guwolsan

Im Kkeokjeong was born some sixty years after Hong Gildong. He was a wicker worker in Yangju, Gyeonggi-do Province, and therefore part of the much-scorned *cheonmin* social class.

For a three-year period beginning in 1559, Im was active across Pyeongan-do and Gangwon-do provinces and even as far as Hanyang. His base was at Mt. Guwolsan,

Chiljangsa Temple
Located in Anseong, Gyeonggi-do Province, this temple is associated with a story of Im Kkeokjeong. Im is said to have come here to see his teacher, the Great Master Byeonghae, who was a leather shoe-maker turned monk. Legends about Later Goguryeo king Gungye and the undercover royal inspector Park Munsu are also connected to Chiljangsa. On the outer walls of the temple's Myeongbujeon Hall are murals illustrating the legends of Gungye and Im Kkeokjeong.

in Hwanghae-do Province. Im specialized in robbing the houses of tyrannical *yangban* and greedy rich people, as well as intercepting various valuable shipments of goods on their way to the capital.

The royal court tried everything it could think of to catch Im, but in vain. Eventually, it sent out a punitive expedition to hunt him down.

One day, Seo Rim, one of Im's advisors, was caught. Nam Chigeun, head of the government expedition, won Seo over to his side and persuaded him to play a leading role in catching the master-bandit.

Eventually, government forces surrounded Im's hideout on Mt. Guwolsan. Nam ordered that every building in the area be searched high and low. At this point, Im entered the home of an old woman and coerced her into raising a false alarm.

Following his orders, she ran out of the house:

"Thief! Thief! He went that way!"

As the government troops charged off in the direction indicated by the old woman, Im took advantage of the confusion by slipping into their ranks, dressed in an army uniform. Just as he was preparing to sneak off and make his escape, Seo recognized him:

"That's him! It's Kkeokjeong!"

Im Kkeokjeong, the bandit of Mt. Guwolsan
Im, a wicker worker of *baekjeong* status, was active across Hwanghae-do, Pyeongan-do, Gangwon-do and Gyeonggi-do provinces, where he robbed greedy officials and *yangban*.

Goseokjeong
Goseokjeong is the name of the pavilion on the left of this photo. It is located in Cheorwon, Gangwon-do Province. Im Kkeokjeong built a wall of stones on the opposite bank of the river and used it as his hideout. While based here, he would steal consignments of tribute on their way to Hanyang and distribute the proceeds among the poor.

Immediately, Im found himself surrounded on all sides by government troops. He breathed his last while pierced by so many arrows that he looked like a porcupine.

Im himself was dead, but his memory lived on with the people, who passed on his legend by word of mouth.

Like that of Hong Gildong, Im's story was written into a novel, this time by a writer named Hong Myeonghui during the Japanese colonial period. I recommend you read it if you get the chance, it's very interesting.

Jang Gilsan, the former entertainer

Well, now it's time for Jang Gilsan. Jang appeared around 130 years later than Im Kkeokjeong and was originally an entertainer. Like *baekjeong*, entertainers lay at the bottom of the social pile in Joseon.

Jang Gilsan as seen by Yi Ik
In his work *Seongho saseol* ("Seongho's Encyclopedic Discourse"), Silhak scholar Yi Ik, who named Hong Gildong, Im Kkeokjeong and Jang Gilsan the "Three Great Bandits of Joseon," described Jang as follows: "In the time of King Sukjong, Jang Gilsan ran amok in Hwanghae-do Province. Gilsan, an entertainer by trade, was a skilled acrobat and a brave man. He therefore became a ringleader among thieves." Yi Ik, too, was a *yangban* and therefore regarded Jang as nothing more than a bandit leader.

Jang, like Im, was based at Mt. Guwolsan in Hwanghae-do Province and active in Pyeongan-do, Gangwon-do and Hamgyeong-do.

He began his career as a righteous thief during the reign of King Sukjong. The royal annals from this period tell how Jang joined forces with a monk from Mt. Geumgangsan named Unbu, gathered followers and invaded Hanyang as part of a secret plan to found a new state. A conspiracy of this

 ## Hwanghae-do Province: a hotbed of banditry

Both Im Kkeokjeong and Jang Gilsan were actively largely in Hwanghae-do Province. Why was this?

Hwanghae-do contained a corridor through which Joseon envoys passed on their way to China, and again on their way back. Each time an envoy passed through, the locals had to provide all kinds of goods as they waited on him and his entourage.

This province, moreover, had to send a much wider variety of specialty products as tribute to the king, and these were subject to more rigorous standards than elsewhere. Deer, among the tribute items demanded, were especially difficult to hunt.

This higher tax burden made life for the commoners of Hwanghae-do particularly hard, which is why the region produced so many bandits.

Tightrope walker
Jang Gilsan was an entertainer, like the tightrope walker in this picture. Entertainers were of *cheonmin* status, the lowest in Joseon society.

scale suggests that Jang was a very bold bandit who wanted nothing less than to take the whole country for himself.

The royal court sent several expeditions to catch Jang, failing each time. Unlike Hong Gildong and Im Kkeokjeong before him, he managed to evade government forces to the end. He was highly adept at covering his tracks and vanishing.

According to legend, Jang made his way to the region of Mt. Baekdusan, right up in the far northeast of Joseon, and founded a village free from discrimination where *yangban* and *cheonmin* lived together in harmony and equality.

Jang Gilsan's story, too, was adapted as an eponymous novel by contemporary writer Hwang Sokyong. I had great fun reading it in my student days.

Politics makes ordinary commoners into thieves

Hong Gildong, Im Kkeokjeong and Jang Gilsan all had one thing in common: officials at the royal court branded them heinous bandits, while commoners considered them to be righteous thieves. But why would anybody have thought such men righteous?

Commoners at the time despised the powerful and greedy government officials that ran roughshod over them. Seeing men like Hong, Im and Jang attacking and robbing such

'Writ' issued by a band of righteous thieves

The band of righteous thieves, known in Korean as the Hwalbindang, was led by Hong Gildong in Heo Gyun's novel. Around 1903, some 300 years after the novel was published, a real "*hwalbindang*" appeared. Regarding themselves as the descendants of Hong Gildong's own band, its members sent "writs" to rich Koreans, demanding money. This writ was sent by the group to Jeong Inwon, a wealthy man in Chungcheong-do Province, to demand the sum of 5,000 *nyang*. It was discovered by chance in a used bookstore a few years ago.

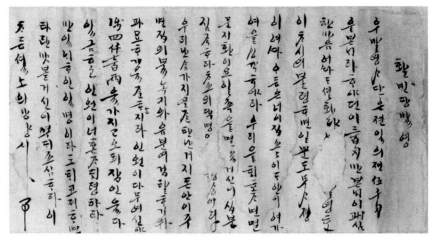

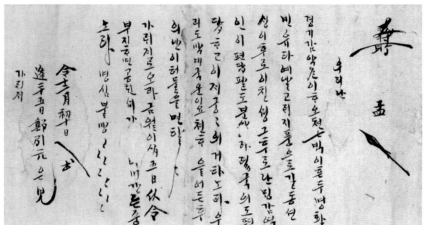

figures, then, while slightly unnerving on one hand, was also highly gratifying.

Commoners would have regarded Hong, Im and Jang as righteous thieves fighting back on behalf of the weak. The fact that all three men had started off from the same humble positions only reinforced this impression. Whether they actually were righteous was not that important to the commoners. What really mattered was the popular longing for such figures.

The ruling class at the time, too, was not unaware of the reasons that such bandits kept emerging. The royal annals contain the following passage:

"The lack of enlightened government from the state is such that the tyranny of ministers and viciousness of local officials are grinding the people into the ground and bleeding them dry. They are left with nowhere to turn as they suffer from starvation and cold, with nothing to eat. They therefore roam around and eventually turn to banditry. This is not their fault: bad government is to blame."

Even the ruling class at the time attributed the proliferation of bandits to political failures that brought hardship to the lives of commoners.

The mysterious tale of Hong Gildong

The Tale of Hong Gildong, written by Heo Gyun during the reign of King Seonjo, is known as the first novel to have been written in Hangeul. It tells the story of how Hong is born the son of a concubine, suffers discrimination as a result, and goes on to become a righteous bandit. Leading the Hwalbindang, he is arrested but later regains his freedom and goes on to become king of a country called Yuldoguk.

A closer look at the novel, however, reveals a strange passage: it occurs at the point when Hong Gildong is complaining that, as the son of a concubine, he is not even allowed to address his own father as "father," or his own brother as "brother." After being scolded by the former for complaining, Hong runs to his mother and announces that he has decided to leave home: "In the olden days, when Jang Chung's son, Gilsan, was born into such low status, he left his mother and went to Mt. Unbongsan..."

Here, "Jang Chung's son, Gilsan" is a reference to none other than Jang Gilsan, the bandit active during the reign of King Sukjong. Jang was around some eighty years after the death of Heo Gyun. How, then, could he have appeared in Heo's novel?

Various scholars are still trying to solve this mystery. Of the theories put forward so far, the most convincing holds that the version of the novel we have today is not the original story written by Heo Gyun himself. In other words, Heo's original *Tale of Hong Gildong* has been lost and the novel that has survived is a version with parts amended or rewritten later on, by somebody else. Some scholars, meanwhile, speculate that Heo's original

'The Tale of Hong Gildong'
This work is famous as the first novel written in Hangeul and for its criticisms of social problems of its time. Some, however, claim that the version that survives today is different to Heo Gyun's original story.
– National Museum of Korea

novel was written in classical Chinese and translated into Hangeul later on. As evidence, they point out that Heo wrote several other novels, all of which are in classical Chinese.

CHAPTER 11

A time of crisis: Japan invades

"All our so-called officials are busy trying to save their own skins. they don't give a damn about the country. That's why men like me, hidden away in the countryside, have to step forward. My ancestors have earned their living from the state for generations, so I'm quite prepared to give my life fighting the enemy."

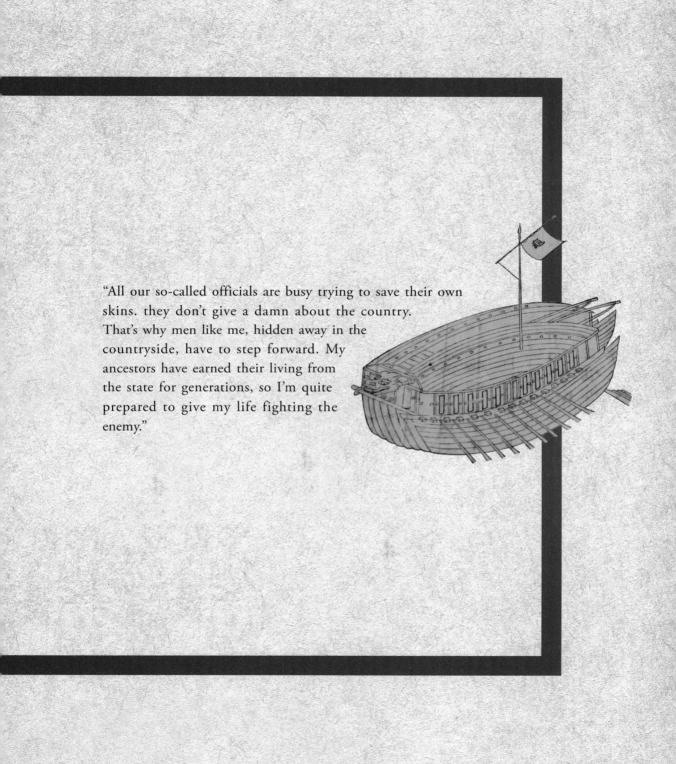

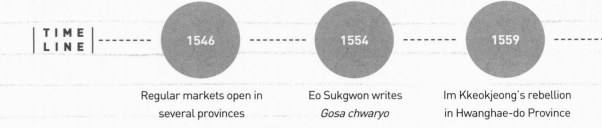

TIME LINE

1546 — Regular markets open in several provinces

1554 — Eo Sukgwon writes *Gosa chwaryo*

1559 — Im Kkeokjeong's rebellion in Hwanghae-do Province

Have you ever heard of the Mimizuka? It's a huge burial mound in kyoto, with a name that literally means "ear mound." In front of it is a sign with the following inscription:

"The ears and noses of Joseon men and women were cut off, salted, brought to Japan and buried here."

The Mimizuka is where trophy parts cut from the bodies of Koreans killed by invading Japanese soldiers are buried. Japanese troops mutilated dead Koreans in this way in order to prove the number of people they had killed. At first, they would take entire heads, but these were hard to carry around because of their size and weight, so they changed to ears. But when some soldiers started cutting off both ears of single victims and claiming that they were from two different people in order to double their recorded number of kills, they were instructed to bring back noses instead. The Minizuka, then, contains not only ears but also noses.

Ear mounds are found in several places, not just kyoto. The total number of buried ears and noses is more than 100,000, which shows just how cruel the Japanese invasions were. Let's have a look at how they started.

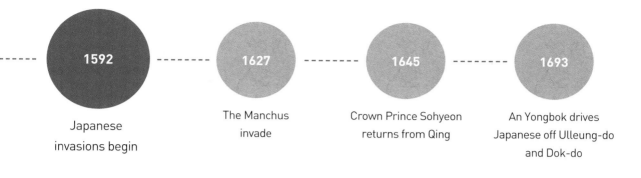

1592
Japanese
invasions begin

1627
The Manchus
invade

1645
Crown Prince Sohyeon
returns from Qing

1693
An Yongbok drives
Japanese off Ulleung-do
and Dok-do

Two hundred years had passed since Taejo Yi Seonggye founded Joseon. By now, the country had acquired solid foundations. The king and government officials ruled through systems based on Neo-Confucianism, while the people were gradually getting used to the new state. Several bloody *sahwa* purges had taken place as a result of power struggles among the ruling class. The latter itself had been challenged by figures such as Hong Gildong and Im Kkeokjeong, who were branded righteous thieves by the people for their efforts. On the whole, though society operated peacefully from one day to the next without ever being seriously destabilized.

Mimizuka
This "ear mound" is located in Kyoto right next to Toyokuni Shrine, which honors Toyotomi Hideyoshi. At the top of the mound is a pagoda. Ethnic Koreans living in Japan often leave Roses of Sharon, the national flower of Korea, in front of the tomb.

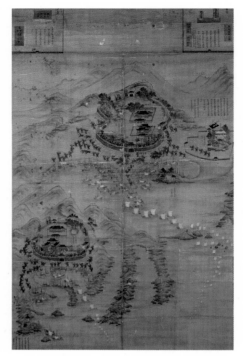

Imjin jeollando
In April, 1592, a Japanese army of 200,000 attacked the coast of Busan. The Joseon forces guarding fought as hard as they could, but were all killed.
–Kyujanggak Institute for Korean Studies

One day, however, the people of Joseon suddenly found themselves swept up in the maelstrom of war. Japan had invaded. In April, 1592, 200 years after the founding of Joseon, the so-called Imjin War began (*imjin* was the calendar name of 1592). Why did Japan invade? It's often said that Toyotomi Hideyoshi, the man who unified it, started a war in order to distract his potential rivals by concentrating their energe on a conflict abroad. Some say there was another reason, too: Japan wanted to trade with Joseon but kept being rebuffed, prompting it to resort to coercive methods. I think this second opinion makes sense.

Gyeongbokgung in flames

On April 14, 1592, Japan invaded Korea with a huge army of 200,000 men. Appearing suddenly off the coast of Busan, the Japanese forces took the city in no time at all and started pushing their way up towards the capital with startling speed. Hanyang fell in less than a month, followed by Pyongyang in less than two.

Just before Hanyang fell into enemy hands, King Seonjo and his leading court officials fled to the north. As soon as the king had left the capital, Gyeongbokgung Palace was burned down. So who was responsible?

Some say the city's *nobi* had set fire to the Office of Slave Registry, which contained all the documents relating to their captivity, and that the flames then spread to the rest of the palace; others claim the fire was started by Japanese forces. In any case, Gyeongbokgung, once the pride of Joseon, was now a smoldering pile of ashes.

Fleeing the capital, Seonjo and his officials met with a frosty reception from the commoners they encountered. The king's sons, Prince Imhae and Prince Sunhwa, who had been dispatched to Hamgyeong-do Province to recruit soldiers, found no response from the locals and were taken prisoner by the Japanese after a desperate struggle.

The royal army, meanwhile, kept running away without even attempting to fight. It was "righteous armies," then, that ended up defending Joseon at a time when the country's survival hung by a thread. Have you ever heard of them? They were bands of commoners who came together voluntarily to fight the invaders.

Righteous armies began as groups of Koreans seeking to defend their own hometowns. The *yangban*, peasants and *nobi* living in a particular area would gather and create a righteous army unit, led by a renowned local *yangban*.

Tomb of Seven Hundred Patriotic Martyrs
This is the resting place of Jo Heon, Yeonggyu Daesa and the approximately 700 men who died in battle against the Japanese. Their remains were gathered and buried in this single, large tomb. It is located in Geumsan, Chungcheongnam-do Province.
–Chilbaeguichong Shrine Office

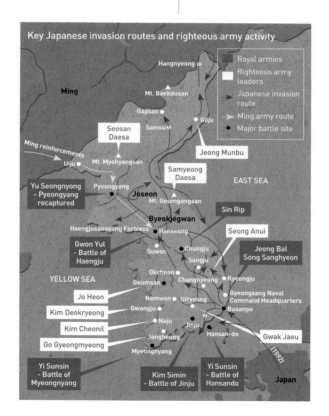

Key Japanese invasion routes and righteous army activity

Royal armies
Righteous army leaders
Japanese invasion route
Ming army route
Major battle site

Hangnyeong
Ming
Mt. Baekdusan
Gapsan
Gilju
Samsu
Seosan Daesa
Jeong Munbu
Ming reinforcements
Uiju
Mt. Myohyangsan
Samyeong Daesa
EAST SEA
Yu Seongnyong - Pyeongyang recaptured
Pyeongyang
Joseon
Mt. Geumgangsan
Byeokjegwan
Sin Rip
Haengjusanseong Fortress
Hanseong
Seong Anui
Gwon Yul - Battle of Haengju
Suwon
Chungju
Sangju
Jeong Bal Song Sanghyeon
YELLOW SEA
Okcheon
Changnyeong
Kyeongju
Geumsan
Gyeongsang Naval Command Headquarters
Jo Heon
Namwon
Uiryeong
Busanpo
Kim Deokryeong
Gwangju
Kim Cheonil
Naju
Jinju
Go Gyeongmyeong
Jangheung
Hansan-do
Gwak Jaeu
Myeongnyang
(1592)
Yi Sunsin - Battle of Myeongnyang
Kim Simin - Battle of Jinju
Yi Sunsin - Battle of Hansando
Japan

Righteous armies take the lead

During the Mongol invasions of the Goryeo period, the king and his ministers fled to Ganghwa-do Island but the commoners formed their own armies and fought back against the Mongols, then the world's most powerful military force. Now, more than 350 years on, the people once again did their best to defend their own villages. Launching repeated attacks from all sides, they stalled the progress of the invaders. Righteous armies formed all over the country; those led by Gwak Jaeu, Kim Cheonil, Go Gyeongmyeong and Jo Heon are the most famous today.

These are the words of Gwak, a student of Neo-Confucian scholar Jo Sik, as he stepped forward to encourage the righteous armies:

"All our so-called officials are busy trying to save their own skins: they don't give a damn about the country. That's why men like me, hidden away in the countryside, have to step forward. My ancestors have earned their living from the state for generations, so I'm quite prepared to give my life fighting the enemy."

Gwak put all his money into gathering men and forming a righteous army. He put on a uniform of red silk and began calling himself the "General in Red."

Jo Heon, a student of Yi I, also formed a righteous army in Okcheon, Chungcheong-do Province. He led some 700 men into battle against the Japanese at Geumsan, but was killed fighting.

Kim Cheonil faced a Japanese army at Jinjuseong Fortress. Even when his men were out of arrows and their metal spears all broken, they carried on fighting with sharpened bamboo stems. Despite their efforts, however, Jinjuseong fell into enemy hands. Kim and his son took their own lives by jumping into the Namgang River.

Bands of monk-soldiers also fought bravely. Normally, Buddhist clergymen regarded all life as precious and went out of their way not to kill so much as a fly; now, though, they headed into battle to save their country from crisis. Their armies were led by famous monks such as Seosan Daesa, Samyeongdang and Yeonggyu.

Turtle ships come into their own

In addition to the righteous armies, Yi Sunsin's naval forces secured victories for Joseon. So-called "turtle ships," in particular, found a place at the heart of the action, inflicting

Peace treaty conditions proposed by Japan
One: Ming sends a princess to marry the Japanese emperor. Two: Bilateral trade is revived. Three: Ministers from Japan and Ming exchange vows of friendship. Four: Hanyang and the four Joseon provinces to the north of the capital are returned to Joseon, while the four southern provinces go to Japan. Five: In exchange for getting the upper four provinces back, Joseon sends a prince and ministers to Japan as hostages. Six: The captured Joseon princes, Imhae and Sunhwa, are sent back to Joseon. Seven: Joseon ministers vow not to betray Japan.

'Crane wing formation'
This tactic was used by Admiral Yi Sunsin at the Battle of Hansan-do. Battleships were arranged in a "U" shape similar to the extended wings of a crane. Turtle ships charged at the enemy's fleet, creating confusion, while other battleships within the formation fired their cannons continuously.

heavy damage on the Japanese fleet thanks to their high maneuverability. Joseon's naval victories severed supply lines that were vital for delivering food and other goods to invading troops in Korea — a heavy blow to the Japanese.

Around this time, reinforcements sent from Ming arrived in Joseon. Led by General Li Rusong, they won back Pyeongyang and pushed the Japanese down as far as Byeokjegwan, to the north of Seoul. Here, though, they were defeated and retreated back to Pyeongyang. The invaders now besieged Haengjusanseong Mountain Fortress. 2,300 Joseon troops under the command of Gwon Yul fought fiercely with a Japanese army of some 30,000, eventually repelling it. This was the famous clash now known as the Battle of Haengjusanseong Fortress.

With the tide turning against them, the Japanese attempted to reach a peace agreement with Ming. The Chinese empire, too, wanted a peace deal to avoid dragging the war out any longer. Talks began in April, 1593. Though the war had been fought on Korean soil, the negotiations took place between representatives of Ming and Japan only, with Koreans excluded.

Japan proposed seven conditions for peace, which Ming

Antonio Corea

More than thirty years ago, in 1983, a painting by famous seventeenth-century artist Peter Paul Rubens titled *Man in Korean Costume* was sold for a very large sum at an art auction house in England. It subject was a handsome man dressed smartly in *hanbok*. So who was he, and how did he become Rubens's model?

At the time of the Japanese invasions, an Italian merchant named Francesco Carletti was in Japan. Joseon subjects brought back as prisoners of war were being sold as slaves, and Carletti bought five young boys. Later, upon arriving in India, he set four of them free, taking only the brightest with him to Italy. This boy became known as Antonio Corea. He appears in Carletti's book, *My Voyage Around the World*, in which the author writes, "He now lives in Rome." It turns out that Rubens, too, was living in Rome at this time. Surely, then, the "man in Korean costume" painted by Rubens must depict Antonio Corea.

Not only Corea but a great many others were abducted from Joseon and taken to Japan during the invasions. Their descendants are probably spread across the world, even if we don't know exactly who they are. A small village in southern Italy by the name of Albi is home to a large number of people with the surname Corea. Could they be the descendants of Antonio? We have no way of knowing for certain.

Rubens's 'Man in Korean Costume'
Who is this man dressed in *hanbok*? Could it be Antonio Corea, the Joseon man abducted during the Japanese invasions?

The Battle of Haengju
This encounter was won thanks to new weapons such as *singijeon* (rocket-propelled arrows) and *hwacha* (multiple rocket launcher), and thanks to the strong solidarity among the Joseon forces, from top generals down to commoners.
– The War Memorial of Korea

considered too absurd even to contemplate. Ultimately, the peace talks fell apart.

The second Japanese invasion

After its negotiations with Ming collapsed, Japan invaded Joseon once again. This second war is known as the Jeongyu Jaeran, literally meaning "second disturbance of the year *jeongyu*." This time, Japanese forces concentrated their attacks on Jeolla-do Province, an area they had failed to reach during the first invasion.

At the time, Yi Sunsin was in prison for having disobeyed royal orders. In his place, a man named Won Gyun had been appointed commander-in-chief of the naval forces of the south. Faced with a large Japanese fleet, Won advocated a

● **Weapons used during the Japanese invasions**

'Singijeon'
(rocket-propelled arrows)

'Hwacha'
(multiple rocket launcher)

Rifles

'Singijeon' arrows loaded into a 'hwacha' launcher

joint land and sea operation. But his commander-in-chief, Gwon Yul, ignored this recommendation and beat Won with a club, telling him to go out and fight. Won had no choice but to obey, and was killed at the Battle of Chilcheollyang.

Jindo-daegyo Bridge and Uldolmok
The narrow strait crossed by this bridge is Uldolmok, the site of one of Yi Sunsin's greatest victories.

When Yi Sunsin was released and put back in charge of the southern naval forces, he found only twelve ships left. Nonetheless, using the local tides to his advantage, he managed with his dozen vessels to fight off some 130 Japanese ships and retake the coast of Jeolla-do. This incident is now known as the Battle of Myeongnyang.

Myeongnyang, also known as Uldolmok, is a narrow stretch of water that separates Jin-do Island from Haenam, on the southwest coast of Korea. Turbulent, fast-flowing and treacherous, the strait is now spanned by Jindo-daegyo Bridge.

In 1598, Hideyoshi died of an illness in Japan and his troops began pulling out of Joseon. The hardest part of their withdrawal was passing through Jeolla-do Province, where they met Yi Sunsin's forces. Together with Ming general Chen Lin, Yi launched a huge onslaught on the retreating invaders at Noryang. It was here that he was killed in battle.

Battle of Bukgwan memorial
This stele was erected in memory
of the righteous soldiers and their
leader, Jeong Munbu, who fought
in Hamgyeong-do Province during
the Japanese invasions. The stele
was taken to Japan around 1904 and
only returned to Joseon in October,
2005. More than a hundred years
after its removal, a joint campaign
by North and South Korea finally
succeeded in bringing it back. After
standing for a while in the grounds
of Gyeongbokgung Palace, the stele
was finally sent to North Korea in
March, 2006, to be returned to its
original place.

Later that year, the last Japanese forces finally left Busan. Seven years of war had come to an end, leaving Joseon devastated. Countless commoners had been killed or abducted, while much of the country's cultural heritage had been burned to ashes or taken to Japan. Jongmyo Shrine and other buildings of national importance had been incinerated, a fate shared by most of the country's most valuable history books.

Many potters and other craftsmen had been taken off to Japan. Figures such as Yi Sampyeong, known today as the godfather of Japanese pottery, and Sim Danggil, the first man to produce the world-renowned Satsuma ware, were Joseon potters kidnapped at this time. Thanks to Joseon craftsmen like Yi and Sim, Japanese pottery made huge advances. This is why the Japanese invasions are sometimes also called the "pottery wars."

The conflicts produced significant international reverberations. In Japan, Tokugawa Ieyasu succeeded Hideyoshi as the country's supreme leader. Ming, meanwhile, gradually grew weaker after sending so many men to fight in Joseon, and was eventually destroyed by Qing.

Were turtle ships really clad in iron?

Though nobody, of course, believes it today, turtle ships were once said to have been the world's first submarines. If this were the case, they would naturally have been clad in iron in order to allow them to operate underwater. But it has already been established that turtle ships weren't submarines. Were they even clad in iron, then?

The turtle ship replicas once moored on the Hangang River in Seoul and now relocated to Tongyeong, on the south coast, and the miniature models you find in gift shops, all feature iron cladding.

Doesn't that seem a bit strange, though? Iron is much heavier than wood—surely this would have adversely affected the ship's speed, which was its greatest strength. Iron would have rusted quickly with so much exposure to rain and seawater, and it was expensive.

Not one word about iron-clad ships is to be found in all the writings of Yi Sunsin and those close to him. When describing his turtle ships to the king, Yi said he had "planted sharp spikes on the upper part." Yi's nephew, Yi Bun, said, "The upper part was covered with boards, into which were stuck sharp spikes everywhere but on a few narrow pathways to allow people to move around."

In other words, the upper part of each turtle ship was covered with spiked boards. Surely these would have been made of wood, rather than iron? Since no authentic drawing of a turtle ship remains, this mystery is hard to solve.

Turtle ship
Turtle ships were similar in appearance to *panokseon* (literally "board-roofed ships"), the vessels normally used by the Joseon navy. The difference was that *panokseon* had flat decks, whereas turtle ships were covered by rounded canopies. This photo shows an image found in *Yi Chungmu Gong jeonseo* ("Collected Works of Admiral Yi Sunsin"), published during the reign of King Jeongjo. *Panokseon* and turtle ships played vital roles during the Japanese invasions.

CHAPTER 12

Fighting off the Manchus

Injo was made to approach the platform on which the emperor sat. He walked over with a hundred steps, then prostrated himself at the bottom of the stairs, bowing as a sign of surrender. He bowed three times, each time so deeply that his forehead touched the ground three times. This demonstration of deep respect was known as *sanbai koutou*, a term that is the source of the English word "kowtow." Joseon thus became a vassal of Qing. What a sad, shameful scene!

How did the country reach this point? And why had Qing invaded?

TIME
LINE

1546

Regular markets open in
several provinces

1554

Eo Sukgwon writes
Gosa chwaryo

1559

Im Kkeokjeong's rebellion
in Hwanghae-do Province

If you know that Japan was commonly referred to in Korea as Wae, it should make sense to you that the Japanese invasions are known as Waeran, literally meaning "Japanese disturbances." But when Koreans talk about Horan, which country was the source of the trouble?

The Sino-Korean word "ho" means "barbarian." This is how Joseon regarded the Manchus, a northern people also known as the Jurchen. Coming, naturally enough, from Manchuria, the Manchus founded China's Qing dynasty. The new state was originally named Later Jin, but subsequently became known as Qing. But I'll use the latter name from the start, for the sake of convenience.

Just as the Waeran took place twice, one in the year imjin *and one in the year* jeongyu, *so did the Horan: the first in the year* jeongmyo *(1627) and the second in the year* byeongja *(1636). While the Japanese invasions dragged on for a whole seven years, the Manchu incursions lasted no more than around forty days each. The latter, however, caused just as much damage as the former. Today, let's find out more about Joseon's wars with Qing.*

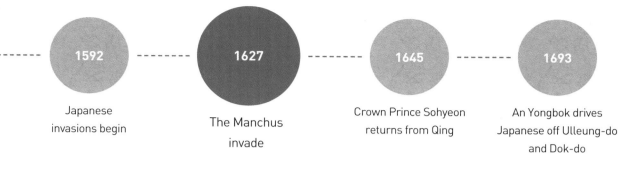

1592
Japanese invasions begin

1627
The Manchus invade

1645
Crown Prince Sohyeon returns from Qing

1693
An Yongbok drives Japanese off Ulleung-do and Dok-do

On January 30, 1637, a cold winter's day, King Injo, Crown Prince Sohyeon and some 50 attendants stepped out of the gate of Namhansanseong Mountain Fortress, where they had been taking refuge. The fog that day was thick enough to hide the sun. When they reached

Nammun Gate, Namhansanseong Mountain Fortress
Injo and his ministers fled here during the second Manchu invasion. In the end, though, they emerged again on a cold winter's day and headed to Samjeon Ferry Point, where they surrendered to Hong Taiji.

The 'three kneelings and nine kowtows'
This act of respect had to be performed by all subjects who came before the emperor. It consists of three deep bows, during each of which the forehead must touch the ground three times.

Samjeon Ferry Point at Songpa, where the Qing army had struck camp, the emperor, Hong Taiji, was already waiting for them.

Hong sat on a high platform, a flight of nine steps up from the ground. His position was deliberately raised, forcing anyone standing before it to look up. His yellow tent and parasol were splendid to behold. Surrounding the emperor on all sides were tens of thousands of warriors, clad in armor and carrying weapons. Qing imperial banners fluttered in the wind.

Injo was made to approach the platform on which the emperor sat. He walked over with a hundred steps, then prostrated himself at the bottom of the stairs, bowing as a sign of surrender. He bowed three times, each time so deeply that his forehead touched the ground three times. This

King Injo and his retinue on the way to Samjeon Ferry Point
Joseon ministers follow their king, choking back their tears. Injo was forced to kowtow before Hong Taiji, the Qing emperor.

demonstration of deep respect was known as sanbai koutou, a term that is the source of the English word "kowtow." Joseon thus became a vassal of Qing. What a sad, shameful scene!

How did the country reach this point? And why had Qing invaded? Let's go back to when the hostilities first began.

King Gwanghaegun's wise policy of neutrality

At this time, Qing was the rival of Ming, China's ruling dynasty. Based in Manchuria, it was waiting for the right chance to topple Ming and achieve dominance in China. If we compare Ming at this point to an aging tiger with no teeth, Qing was like a young leopard with boundless energy. It was clearly only a matter of time before the latter brought down the former and took possession of China. If you had been king of Joseon at this point, which side would you have taken?

Qing, surely, would seem the obvious choice, since Ming was on the verge of collapsing. That's also what King Gwanghaegun of Joseon thought. But Ming urged Joseon to send troops and help it fight against the Manchus, pointing out that it had helped Joseon during the Japanese invasions. Qing, meanwhile, promised to leave Joseon alone as long as it pledged not to cooperate with Ming, its sole target.

Samjeondo Stele
The official name of this stele is Daqing Huangdi Gongde Bei, meaning "Stele [Listing] the Good Deeds of the Great Qing Emperor." It was erected by Hong Taiji after he had secured Joseon's surrender. The inscription on it appears in three languages: Chinese, Mongol and Manchu. The stele now stands in Seokchon-dong, Songpa-gu, Seoul

'Hanghae jocheondo'
This painting shows a Joseon envoy and his entourage traveling by sea to Ming. "*Jocheon*" means "paying respect to the heavenly emperor."
– National Museum of Korea

Gwanghaegun's ministers were divided. While some believed Joseon still owed Ming a debt of gratitude from the days of the Japanese invasions, others believed it more important not to rub up Qing the wrong way. Those who supported Ming regarded Qing as a nation of barbarians.

Facing such complicated circumstances, Gwanghaegun took a very wise stance. He responded to Ming that Joseon had only just finished fighting off the Japanese, leaving it completely unready to send troops. At the same time, he explained to Qing Joseon's difficult position, whereby it was difficult to simply ignore Ming's requests. In so doing, the king had chosen a policy of diplomatic neutrality that offended neither party. Rather than taking one particular side and being dragged into a fight, he wanted to benefit his country by keeping a reasonable distance from both.

Eventually, however, Gwanghaegun could no longer refuse Ming's requests and dispatched forces. He sent off General Gang Hongnip with 10,000 men and a top secret order:

"Wait for the right moment, then surrender to Qing, telling them we only sent troops because Ming kept pushing us, and that we've no intention of fighting them. Tell them we don't see them as enemies. I'll take care of whatever happens after that."

"Your majesty, it will be my honor to carry out your royal order."

Gang faithfully followed the king's instructions. As a result, the flames of the Ming-Qing conflict stayed out of Joseon and the country avoided further disaster.

Gwanghaegun's brand of neutral diplomacy was needed more than ever at the time: the most pressing task for Joseon was not loyalty to Ming but repairing the damage caused by the Japanese invasions and restoring a public sense of stability.

Gang Hongnip surrenders
This image shows Gang and his Joseon army being given a lavish welcome by Emperor Nurhaci of Qing after surrendering. The inscription in Chinese on the left reads "Gang Hongnip surrendered with all his men." The image and text are taken from *Manzhou shilu*, an illustrated description of the life of Nurhaci.

War begins

Not long afterwards, Gwanghaegun was deposed by

'Hobyeongdo'
This painting by eighteenth-century painter Kim Yungyeom depicts Qing soldiers, giving us a good idea of how they looked and dressed.
– National Museum of Korea

ministers opposed to his neutral diplomacy. These men were members of a faction known as the Westerners, of which we'll see more later on.

The Westerners completed their coup by installing a new king: Injo. Having done so, they took a stance of absolute support for Ming and rejection of Qing, publicly proclaiming their animosity toward the latter and their willingness to help the former. Injo was just the same. Perhaps in order to prove that he was right and Gwanghaegun wrong, the new king was event more strident in his support of Ming and condemnation of Qing.

Qing thus invaded Joseon, aiming to eliminate any potential future risks before it launched an all-out attack on Ming. And guess what pretext it used for this invasion: it claimed to be "avenging Gwanghaegun."

In January, 1627, 30,000 Qing troops crossed the Amnokgang River into Joseon. Like a tidal surge, they swept down to Hwanghae-do in just eleven days. This was the first invasion, known in Korea as the Jeongmyo Horan. Injo and his ministers hurriedly fled to Ganghwa-do Island. Despite their shrill calls for supporting Ming and rejecting Qing, they had done nothing to prepare for an invasion, leaving Joseon completely vulnerable.

Driven into a corner, Injo suggested a peace agreement.

Qing agreed, wanting to get the war over with as soon as possible, and accepted a promise from Joseon to become its "younger brother." For Joseon, which had dismissed Qing as a nation of barbarians, being forced to make such a vow was deeply humiliating.

Joseon did not keep its promise. Therefore, in December, 1936 — some ten years later — Qing invaded again. This second invasion is known as the Byeongja Horan. This time, Qing sent a great army of 100,000 men. After just six days, they had taken Hanyang. Injo, after attempting to flee to Ganghwa-do once again but finding his path blocked, took refuge in Namhansanseong Mountain Fortress.

Layer upon layer of Qing forces now laid siege to the fortress. Inside, an argument broke out between those in favor of fighting and those who advocated suing for peace.

Sueojangdae, Namhansanseong Mountain Fortress
Together, Namhansanseong and Bukhansanseong mountain fortresses guarded Hanyang to the north and south. Namhansanseong was completed in 1626, just before the first Manchu invasion.

But Joseon lacked both the strength and the preparation to fight, even if it had wanted to.

Injo and his retinue walked to Samjeon Ferry Point, where the king performed the three kneelings and nine kowtows before Qing emperor Hong Taiji. As part of the agreement, Joseon sent Crown Prince Sohyeon, Prince Bongnim and their wives, leading members of the faction who had argued against the peace agreement, and the daughters of ministers to Qing as hostages, as well as promising to support the latter in its conquest of Ming. From then on, Joseon was forced to serve Qing as a vassal state.

Returned prisoners

Just as at the time of the Japanese invasions, countless Joseon citizens were taken away as prisoners by the Manchus planning to ransom them later on for a huge profit. Qing soldiers were desperate to round up as many captives as they could. Wherever possible, they took away *yangban*, who fetched more ransom money than commoners.

Once the war was over, no fewer than 630,000 Joseon prisoners paid ransoms to regain their freedom, which should give you an idea of just how many people Qing forces abducted.

Among those of *yangban* status, however, men and women

Hong Haksa memorial
stele and building
The stele in this building
was erected in honor of
Hong Ikhan, one of three
officials who advocated
fighting Qing forces rather
than surrendering. When
Injo did surrender, the
three officials—Hong, Yun
Jip and O Dalje— were
taken to Qing following
their king's capitulation and
executed on the grounds
that they had been Qing's
leading opponents in the
Joseon court. The Hong
Haksa memorial stele is
located in Pyeongtaek,
Gyeonggi-do Province

were received very differently back in Joseon. The former were welcomed and consoled on account of the hard times they had been through, but the latter were not even allowed back into their own homes, on the grounds that their chastity had been compromised. Countless women died of exhaustion after pleading for days outside the tightly closed gates of their husband's houses, starved to death after wandering around when nobody would take them in, or hanged themselves when they had nowhere left to go. They died for the sole reason that they had been taken prisoners.

Looking back now, it's apparent just how unjustly these women died. They were taken prisoner not through any fault of their own, but because their country's leaders had failed to protect them. But instead of being offered the comfort and

Tomb of Gwanghaegun
Gwanghaegun's resting place is simpler than other royal tombs because he was driven from the throne, and therefore not accorded the same posthumous status as most monarchs. On the left is Gwanghaegun's tomb, while that on the right belongs to his wife, Lady Yu.

compensation they deserved, they were held responsible for what had happened.

The Manchu invasions may have been entirely avoidable: if Gwanghaegun's policy of neutrality had been continued, there would have been no reason for Qing to invade. When you think about the countless people killed and injured in the wars, the unspeakable havoc they wrought and the women who died amid such terrible injustice, this impression grows even stronger.

Oh, and what became of Gwanghaegun after he was deposed? After living out the remainder of his days in exile on Jeju-do Island, he died a lonely death at the age of sixty-seven. In his will, he made the following request:

"When I die, please bury me at the foot of my mother's grave."

In according with his dying wish, Gwanghaegun was buried at the feet of his mother, Lady Kim, at a tomb in today's Namyangju, Gyeonggi-do Province. She was a royal concubine who died when Gwanghaegun was a boy. Because he was dethroned, his name was not accorded either of the normal suffixes for kings, *-jo* or *-jong*, but simply *-gun*.

The difference between '-jo,' '-jong' and '-gun'

Appellations with the suffix *-jo* or *-jong* are not used while a king is still alive. Known as temple names, they are given only after he has died and is enshrined at Jongmyo. Certain criteria existed in the conferring of temple names: those ending in *-jo* were given to kings with particularly great achievements to their names, while those ending in *-jong* were bestowed upon those of great virtue. Yi Seonggye, for example, was posthumously named Taejo because of his achievement in founding Joseon.

Several kings had their temple name suffixes changed to *-jo* after first being given those ending with *-jong*. This was the case with Seonjo, Yeongjo, Jeongjo and Sunjo, whose temple names were originally Seonjong, Yeongjong, Jeongjong and Sunjong. Seonjo's name was changed in recognition of his achievement in defending the dynasty from the Japanese, while Yeongjong, Jeongjong and Sunjong had their names changed due to various particular political circumstances. Kings forced off the throne were given names ending with *-gun*, examples being Yeonsangun and Gwanghaegun.

Kim Sangheon and Choe Myeonggil

When a heated argument broke out among those taking refuge in Namhansanseong over whether to fight against Qing or sue for peace, the leading advocates of peace and war were Choe Myeonggil and Kim Sangheon, respectively. The two men exchanged stinging criticisms.

Kim called Choe a disloyal subject who was trying to save his own skin by sucking up to a bunch of barbarians, while Choe slammed Kim for trying to wreck his own country by ignoring reality and trying to uphold an empty cause.

'Seolgo sicheop,' Kim Sangheon's poetry anthology
Kim Sangheon, who advocated fighting Qing's forces to the end during the second Manchu invasion, was taken prisoner by the Manchus, only returning six years later. He wrote the poems in *Seolgo sicheop* while in captivity in China.

Eventually, Choe wrote a letter to send to Qing, asking for a peace agreement. When he saw this, Kim flew into a rage and tore it up.

"How can a man born as a scholar do something like this?"

Choe picked up the pieces of the letter and laughed as he reassembled it.

"Tear it up if you like, sir. I'll just put it back together again."

Later on, the two men ended up together in a Qing prison, separated by a single wall. Only then, after hating each other for so long, did they finally develop a true mutual understanding. They realized they had both wanted the best for their country, even if their methods had been different, and wrote poems expressing their new-found mutual trust:

I've thought long and hard about both our opinions.

Now I realize I was wrong to call you a traitor.

Choe replied to Kim's words:

Your heart is like a rock, too firm and too heavy to shift.
The path I follow is a winding one; it turns with the lie of the land.

Only now did the two men truly make peace and come to respect each other. Not long afterwards, they were released.

CHAPTER 13

What caused factional strife?

I believe there's no need either to hide the fact that factional strife occurred or to exaggerate what actually happened. And I don't think it's right to liken it to the competition between various political parties in today's democratic society. Surely political parties representing popular opinion in a democracy and the factions formed by officials in a monarchy are fundamentally different?

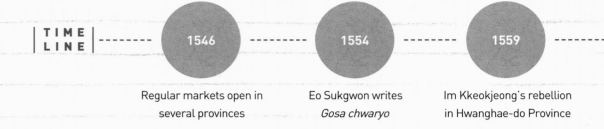

TIME LINE -------- 1546 --------- 1554 --------- 1559 -------------

Regular markets open in
several provinces

Eo Sukgwon writes
Gosa chwaryo

Im Kkeokjeong's rebellion
in Hwanghae-do Province

*If you've ever watched a Korean historical drama on television, you may be familiar
with the problem of factional strife, when ministers became divided and fought among
themselves.*

*But how did these disputes arise? Was it because members of each faction worked in
each other's favor to secure rapid promotion and success?*

*The history of Joseon is often seen as one riddled with factional strife, to the extent
where such conflict is considered a defining feature of the period. But factionalism was
not unique to Joseon: it was found all over the world. And while it's true that factional
strife went on in Joseon, it's not as if the period's entire history is packed full of it.
Joseon is so strongly associated with factional strife because of Japanese historians
during the colonial period, who greatly emphasized and exaggerated factionalism in
the pre-modern state. Why? In order to make the collapse of Joseon due to factionalism
seem inevitable, thus implying that the Japanese occupation was also a natural turn of
events.*

So what view should we really take of factionalism? Let's spend today considering this.

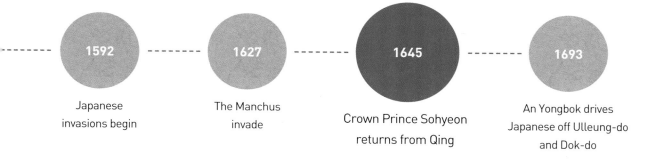

1592 — Japanese invasions begin

1627 — The Manchus invade

1645 — Crown Prince Sohyeon returns from Qing

1693 — An Yongbok drives Japanese off Ulleung-do and Dok-do

What exactly is factional strife? You may recall the *sahwa* literati purges that I mentioned recently: how the meritorious elite faction and the Neo-Confucian literati faction competed for years, with the latter eventually winning. The factional strife I want to talk about today occurred when the Neo-Confucian literati themselves, having reached power, became divided into two camps and started fighting. As I've just said, the factional strife stories with which most Koreans are familiar today were overblown by Japanese historians. How, then, should we really view this phenomenon in the Joseon period?

I believe there's no need either to hide the fact that factional strife occurred or to exaggerate what actually happened. And I don't think it's right to liken it to the competition between various political parties in today's democratic society. Surely political parties representing popular opinion in a democracy and the factions formed by officials in a monarchy are fundamentally different?

The beginnings of factional strife

All this strife began during the reign of King Seonjo, immediately before the Japanese invasions. At this time, officials began taking sides and fighting over appointments to positions in the Ministry of Personnel known as *jeollang*. Though not that high in terms of the the *pumgye* ranking system, these posts were extremely important because of the powers of appointment they carried.

At the time, two men emerged as candidates to fill a vacant *jeollang* position: Kim Hyowon and Sim Chunggyeom, younger brother of Sim Uigyeom. The two men began a highly tense stand-off.

Kim and Sim both lived in Hanyang, the former in Geoncheon-dong in the east of the city and the latter in Jeongneung-dong in the west. Their respective followers therefore came to be known as Easterners and Westerners. And that's how all the factional strife began.

Later on, the Easterners divided again into Southerners and Northerners, and Westerners into the Noron and Soron factions. Then, the Southerners in turn became divided into the "Cheongnam" and "Tangnam" factions, and the Northerners into "Daebuk" and "Sobuk" factions.

In addition to these, numerous other factions kept emerging. The most powerful among them, however, were the Southerners, the Northerners, the Noron and the Soron. Collectively, they were known as the Four Colored Factions.

Many people died unjustly as a result of factional strife. Let me tell you about one of them, Crown Prince Sohyeon. As Injo's eldest son, Sohyeon was next in line for the throne until his sudden death, which remains surrounded by many questions.

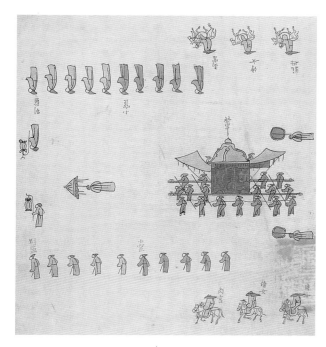

Royal Protocol for the Wedding of Crown Prince Sohyeon
This scene depicts the marriage of the crown prince to Lady Gang. The bride, though invisible, must be sitting in the sedan chair.
–Kyujanggak Institute for Korean Studies

Crown Prince Sohyeon is taken hostage

You will recall how, in my last letter, I wrote how King Injo surrendered to the Qing emperor by kowtowing to him on the banks of the Hangang River. Nine days later, Injo's eldest son, Crown Prince Sohyeon, set off with his wife for Qing. They were being sent as hostages, accompanied by some 180 other

After becoming a hostage of Qing, Sohyeon lived in the city of shenyang in Manchuria. The city is just an hour's flight away from Seoul. At the time, however, it took a whole two months to reach on foot or horseback. While in Shenyang, Sohyeon lived in a building called Shenyang Guansuo, which was shortened to Shenguan. It played a role similar to that of an embassy today, while Sohyeon acted in a capacity similar to that of an ambassador.

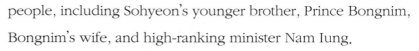

Brass globe
Western science and scholarship came as a huge shock to Crown Prince Sohyeon.
–The Korean Christian Museum at Soongsil University

people, including Sohyeon's younger brother, Prince Bongnim, Bongnim's wife, and high-ranking minister Nam Iung.

Living in a foreign land, Sohyeon had to be careful in everything he did. One mistake could have led to immediate death, or sparked another tumultuous war in Joseon. At the time, moreover, the international political situation was rapidly changing: power in China was transferring from Ming to Qing.

Sohyeon watched intently as Ming, in which Joseon had believed so firmly, collapsed with barely a whimper. He saw that the pro-Ming, anti-Qing stance, for which Joseon had been prepared to fight to the death, was meaningless. And he realized that Qing, which Joseon politicians had labeled barbarian and held in contempt, was actually a genuine superpower with a sophisticated culture.

While in Bejing, Sohyeon got to know a German Jesuit by the name of Johann Adam Schall von Bell. As well as being a Jesuit, Schall von Bell was a scientist. He introduced Sohyeon to Catholicism and Western science and gave him books on Western astronomy, a globe and a Jesus figurine.

How must Sohyeon have felt upon discovering Western culture for the first time? To a man who had studied Neo-Confucianism since childhood and firmly believed it to be the only ideology in the world, it must have been a huge shock to discover that alternatives even existed. He must have been amazed to find that another world, about which he had known absolutely nothing, lay across the sea.

Sohyeon believed the politicians of Joseon also needed to know about this new world. He told Schall von Bell that, once he had returned

'Tianzhu shiyi'
This book, the title of which translates as "The True Meaning of the Lord of Heaven," was written by Italian Jesuit priest Matteo Ricci while he worked as a missionary in China. Ricci, whose grasp of classical Chinese was excellent, wrote the book himself, in Chinese, in order to communicate Catholic doctrine to Chinese readers.
–Catholic University of Korea Museum

to Joseon and become king, he would make the new scholarship and ideology widely known.

At this time, Western science, technology, culture and religion were almost unheard of in Joseon. And since the recent invasions, animosity toward Qing had reached an all-time peak: there was no way that Western culture, entering the country via Qing, could expect a warm welcome.

Johann Adam Schall von Bell
Schall von Bell was a German Jesuit priest and outstanding astronomer.

Sure enough, Joseon's politicians disapproved strongly of Sohyeon. At the time, the Westerners had the upper hand. This was the faction that had driven Gwanghaegun off the throne, in opposition to his neutrality policy. Because the pro-Ming, anti-Qing doctrine was pretty much the only leg they had to stand on, they were totally unable to accept Crown Prince Sohyeon. His father, Injo, took the Westerners' side, since it was their support that had put him on the throne.

Sohyeon returned to Joseon eight years after being taken

hostage by Qing. He was thirty-four years old, and must have been delighted to come home after so long. But his father, Injo, was far from pleased. The story goes that, when Sohyeon showed him the astronomy books and globe he had brought back from Qing and was explaining about Western science and civilization, Injo flew into a rage and hit his son over the head with an ink stone.

This seems rather implausible, don't you think? In any case, Sohyeon suddenly grew ill. The court physician diagnosed malaria and treated him using acupuncture. Nonetheless, the crown prince died just three days later. As he breathed his last, blood was flowing from his ears, eyes, nose and mouth and his face had turned black—typical symptoms of poisoning. Rumors that Sohyeon had not fallen ill but been assassinated began to spread like wildfire.

Sohyeon's family, too, was all but annihilated. His wife, Lady Gang, was condemned to death by drinking poison based on charges that she herself had tried to poison Injo's food. Nobody, however, believed that she was really guilty. Sohyeon's three sons were banished to Jeju-do, where two of them died and the youngest barely managed to survive.

Though Sohyeon's death left many unanswered questions,

Crown Prince Sohyeon returns to Korea
While in Beijing, Crown Prince Sohyeon met German Jesuit priest Johann Adam Schall von Bell, from whom he learned about Western science and culture. The priest gave him Western astronomy books, a globe and a Jesus Christ figurine. When Sohyeon returned to Joseon and showed these things to his father, however, the king flew into a rage and hurled on ink stone at his head.

what's clear is that he didn't simply die from an illness. His failure to achieve harmony with the Westerners, the dominant faction at the time, led to his suspicious demise. He was, to put it simply, a victim of factional strife. If Sohyeon had become king, Joseon would have opened its eyes to Western civilization much earlier, and its history may well have unfolded very differently. His death was a truly sad event.

The fundamental cause of factional strife

What gave rise to factional strife? The basic reason was that, while the number of government positions remained fixed, large numbers of people sought to fill them. Yulgok Yi I, who opposed factional strife, described the situation this way:

"Say you have ten people, all of them starving. You give them one bowl of rice to share, but they start fighting before they've even begun eating."

Anyone seeking a government position would have to develop ties to a particular faction and gain its support. Hopefully, you'll recall how officials were appointed in Joseon. Recommendations were taken, then a shortlist was compiled of individuals with the most recommendations, from which the final candidate was chosen. Once factional strife set in, members of each faction often only recommended candidates from their

Song Siyeol
Song was the head of the Noron faction. He served as a minister under three kings - Hyojong, Hyeonjong and Sukjong - becoming so influential that even the king had to tread carefully around him. Eventually, however, Song was banished to Jeju-do and forced to kill himself by drinking poison after submitting a petition against a plan to make one of the king's sons by a concubine, Lady Jang, a future crown prince.
– National Museum of Korea

own ranks: this is why developing connections to a faction was so important.

Faction membership was intimately linked to factors such as your family background, your place of origin and who your teacher was. Seo Gyeongdeok's students became Easterners, Yi I's Westerners, Yi Hwang's Southerners, Jo Sik's Northerners, and so on.

The two Yis, Jo and Seo themselves had either died before factions came into existence or kept their distance from such matters, so were not directly involved. Rather, it was their students who built factions under their names.

Different factions rose to power at different times. When Gwanghaegun was on the throne, the Northerners were dominant. Under Injo, the Westerners became extremely powerful; they, in turn, were replaced by the Southerners during the reign of Sukjong, until ultimate victory put the Westerners back on top. Remember how I said the Westerners were divided into Noron and Soron factions? Under Yeongjo, the Noron faction held the most power.

Victims of historical slander

The adverse effects of factional strife lasted well beyond the factions themselves. Each victorious faction left historical records that served its best interests. This means that some of the characters portrayed as villains in history books were actually the subjects of smear campaigns. Prime examples are Gwanghaegun, portrayed as a despot; Jeong Yeorip, the reformist thinker branded a traitor; and Sukjong's concubine, Lady Jang. Let me tell you her story.

Lady Jang is widely known as a wicked concubine who

Tombs of King Sukjong and Queen Inhyeon (above) and of Lady Jang (below)
King Sukjong and Queen Inyeon are buried side by side. But Lady Jang, who once rose to the position of queen herself, lies in a solitary tomb known as Daebinmyo. All three tombs are located in the Seooreung complex.

persecuted Queen Inhyeon. All surviving records of the two women were written by Westerners, who supported Inhyeon, while no records written by Jang's supporters, the Southerners, remain.

Jang and Inhyeon lived at a time when factional strife was at its worst. While the Southerners and Westerners competed fiercely for supremacy, Sukjong managed his political affairs by siding with the Westerners at one moment and the Southerners the next—a kind of "divide and rule" strategy.

Inhyeon was queen when Sukjong sided with the Westerners. When he switched sides to the Southerners, however, she was driven out of the palace and Jang promoted to fill her place. When Sukjong once again changed sides and

Jeong Yeorip

Jeong, a member of the Easterners faction, lived in Jukdo, Jeolla-do Province. He believed that the world was public property and could not be owned by any particular person. He also took the view that a king was not a special being: anyone could become monarch and would then be served as such by others. In these respects, Jeong's thinking was well ahead of his time. It was enough to get him arrested, however, and he was later found dead, having killed himself. Around 1,000 other Easterners were killed or punished, too. It is highly likely that the Jeong Yeorip treason incident was fabricated by Westerners in order to topple Easterners from power.

supported the Westerners, Jang was expelled from the palace and Inhyeon restored as queen.

This factional struggle ended with victory for the Westerners. Jang, who was supported by the Southerners, was condemned to death by drinking poison. Inhyeon became queen once again, but died after a protracted illness. Thus it was that the fates of Jang and Inhyeon became entwined in the war between the Westerners and Southerners, fluctuating wildly as the king attempted to preserve his own authority.

Perhaps it's natural that the victorious Westerners portrayed Inhyeon as a kind, benevolent queen and Jang as a wicked, crafty concubine. Thus recorded, these fixed images of the two women remain with us today.

The Impartiality Policy

The Impartiality Policy was introduced in order to eliminate factional strife. Its Korean name, Tangpyeongchaek, comes from a phrase that means "not leaning towards either side." The policy emphasized the need for politics to be conducted with extreme impartiality and rectitude.

King Sukjong was the first to come up with the Impartiality Policy though it was not properly implemented during his reign. Its aim was to weaken the various factions and restore authority to the king himself.

Later on, Yeongjo emphasized the importance of the Impartiality Policy and had an "Impartiality Stele" put up at the entrance to the Royal Confucian Academy. His successor, Jeongjo, also followed the same line. During their reigns, however, it proved insufficient for uprooting factional strife.

Rubbing of the Impartiality Stele
The inscription on this stele reads: "The heart of a gentleman is one of loyalty, not flattery; the mind of a petty individual is one of flattery, not loyalty."

Impartiality Stele
King Yeongjo himself wrote the inscription found on this stele and had it put up at the entrance to the Royal Confucian Academy in 1742 as part of an attempt to emphasize the importance of the impartiality policy. This reflects the fact that the Royal Confucian Academy was a hotbed of factional strife at the time. It is now at the entrance to today's Sungkyunkwan University.

Death in a rice chest: Crown Prince Sado

"Father, please spare me!"

Crown Prince Sado, clutching the edge of a rice chest in a palace courtyard, pleaded with King Yeongjo. Sado's eleven-year-old son (later to become King Jeongjo), cried as he hegged the king to spare his father.

"Who brought him here?" Yeongjo shouted. "Take him out, now!"

A minister grabbed the struggling boy and took him away. Sado had no choice but to get into the chest. Yeongjo then personally closed the lid and fastened the lock. He had wooden boards brought in and nailed them to the chest, before finally sealing it with rope.

Eight days went by. Left in the rice chest under the summer sun, without so much as a drop of water, Sado eventually died. What had he done to earn such a cruel fate? And what had made Yeongjo condemn his own son to death?

Sado is widely believed to have died after showing signs of severe mental illness and falling out of favor with his father. The real reason for his death, however, is intimately connected to factional strife. At the time, the Noron faction had seized power and was in conflict with the Soron. Sado was close to the latter. It was clear that, if he became king, the Noron faction would lose all of its power overnight.

Royal portrait of King Yeongjo
Although Yeongjo promoted a policy of impartiality in government, he ended up leaning towards the Noron faction, which led to the death of his own son, Crown Prince Sado.
– National Palace Museum of Korea

'Hanjungnok'
Written in her later years by Lady Hong, the widow of Crown Prince Sado, this memoir looks back on the events of her life, focusing on the affair that embroiled her husband.
–Kyujanggak Institute for Korean Studies

Keen to prevent this, members of the Noron faction habitually spoke ill of Sado in front of Yeongjo. In the end, his tragic death was the result of fighting between factions.

Yungneung Tomb
This is the tomb of Crown Prince Sado. Joseon tombs were named differently according to the status of their occupants. Those of kings and queens had names that ended with the suffix *-neung*. Those of crown princes, their wives and royal concubines who had given birth to future kings had the suffix *-won*, and all other tombs the suffix *-myo*. Crown Prince Sado's tomb, originally named Hyeollyungwon, became Yungneung once Sado was posthumously granted the status of a king. It is located at Hwaseong in Gyeonggi-do Province.

CHAPTER 14

An Yongbok defends Ulleung-do and Dok-do

In Japan, meanwhile, the general public, with the exception of a handful politicians and others, is largely uninterested in Dok-do. Those few interested people, however, have been remarkable in the detail of their research.

If Koreans want Dok-do to be recognized by the international community as their territory, they need to research the issue more calmly and tenaciously, until they can produce incontrovertible evidence.

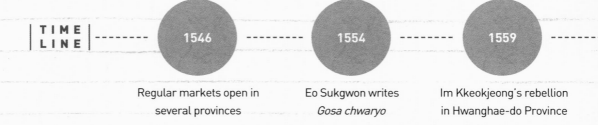

TIME LINE

1546 — Regular markets open in several provinces

1554 — Eo Sukgwon writes *Gosa chwaryo*

1559 — Im Kkeokjeong's rebellion in Hwanghae-do Province

Ask any Korean about which country, Korea or Japan, owns Dok-do Island and he or she will tell you in no uncertain terms that it belongs to the former. Ask why, and many people will be surprised that you could even pose such a question.

It seems the ongoing territorial dispute between Korea and Japan over Dok-do is often driven by emotion. Anyone that bases an argument on feelings this way is likely to end up losing. If Koreans are going to claim Dok-do as their territory, they need to make a logical argument, backed up with clear evidence.

The Dok-do dispute is nothing new. In fact, it existed some 300 years ago, in the Joseon period. In the late seventeenth century, during the reign of King Sukjong, Japan laid claim not only to Dok-do but even to nearby Ulleung-do Island. The man who defended both islands in this dispute was not a famous scholar, politician or general, but an ordinary fisherman from Dongnae in Gyeongsang-do Province named An Yongbok.

Let's see exactly what he did.

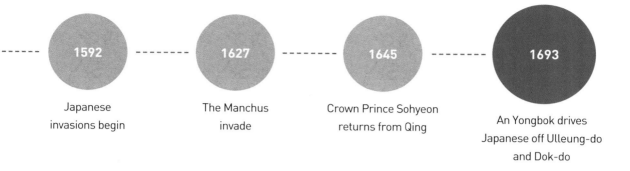

1592	1627	1645	1693
Japanese invasions begin	The Manchus invade	Crown Prince Sohyeon returns from Qing	An Yongbok drives Japanese off Ulleung-do and Dok-do

In spring, 1693, An Yongbok went off with other fishermen to fish in the waters off faraway Ulleung-do. As well as being a fisherman, An was an oarsman in the Joseon navy. They say he spoke excellent Japanese. In his hometown of Dongnae was a *waegwan*, a special facility for accommodating Japanese who came to Korea to trade or on diplomatic business. This would have given An the chance to

A 'waegwan'
Waegwan were built for trading with Japan. This painting is of Choryang Waegwan in Busan.
–National Institute of Korean History

learn their language.

An Yongbok travels to Japan

When he arrived at Ulleung-do, An began fishing with his friend Park Eodun. It was then that they bumped into some Japanese fishermen, who had come all the way to Ulleung-do to fish. The latter took An and Park off to Japan's Oki Islands, accusing them of fishing without permission.

"I'll go where I like in my own country!" An protested strongly. "Why have you brought me here?"

When Tokugawa Tsunayoshi, the Tokugawa shogun, heard about what had happened, he sent An back with a letter saying "Ulleung-do is not Japanese territory."

An and Park set sail for home, stopping at Tsushima on their way. Since all Japanese trading with Joseon at the time had to pass through Tsushima, An was also obliged to do so on his way back to Dongnae. The *daimyo* of Tsushima, however, got greedy and decided to take this opportunity to make Ulleung-do part of Tsushima territory. He locked up An, took his letter away and then lied to the Joseon royal court, saying that An had recklessly trespassed on Japanese territory. Upon his return to Joseon, therefore, An was arrested again and imprisoned in Dongnae, barely managing to escape after three months.

The Joseon navy
An Yongbok was an oarsman in the Joseon navy. All men of commoner status in Joseon had to perform military service between the ages of sixteen and sixty. In the case of the navy, men did compulsory military service for half of every year, in one-month shifts. When they weren't doing military service they would work on farms or fishing boats until it was time for their next shift. That's how life was for commoners in Joseon.

Three years later, An learned that Japanese fishermen were still active in the waters off Ulleung-do and Dok-do. He decided to go back to Japan and have it out with the Japanese. This time, he left for Ulleung-do with the Ven. Noeheon of Songgwangsa Temple in Suncheon, the scholar Yi Inseong, his own wife and sixteen other fishermen.

Sure enough, when they reached Ulleung-do they found Japanese fishing boats at work. An shouted at them:

"Ulleung-do is Korean territory! Why are you Nips trespassing?"

"We live in Song-do," they answered. "We were out fishing and just happened to end up here. We'll go back to Song-do."

"Song-do is Usan-do (another name for Dok-do), which is also Korean territory," An fumed. "How dare you say you live there?"

At dawn the next day, An made his way to Dok-do. The Japanese fisherman he had met the previous day had hung up a big iron pot and were cooking. An took a stick and smashed up their makeshift kitchen. He then pursued the fleeing fishermen all the way to the Oki Islands, where he demanded an explanation from the local official in charge.

"A few years ago, I got a document from the Tokugawa shogun saying that Ulleung-do and Dok-do were Joseon territory," he said. "Why have you invaded our country yet again?"

The official promised to report the matter to his superior, the *daimyo*, but An received no answer, no matter how long he waited. He decided to meet the *daimyo* for himself.

An made a plan to masquerade as the "tax inspector for Ulleung-do and Dok-do." He dressed himself in the shirt, horsehair hat and leather shoes of a high-ranking official and had himself carried in a sedan chair so that he truly looked the part. This way, he hoped to earn some proper respect from the Japanese.

"Last time I was here, I received a letter from the Tokugawa *bakufu* about Ulleung-do and Dok-do," he said. "But on my way back to Joseon the *daimyo* of Tsushima took away the letter and told lies about me. I'll be sure to make a full report of this to the *kampaku*."

Properly scared now, the *daimyo* made An a promise:

"The two islands belong to your country. As such, if anyone from our side trespasses there again, or if the *daimyo* of Tsushima indulges in any more fabrications, I'll be sure to punish them severely."

An and his entourage returned without mishap to Joseon. Two years later, in March, 1698, the Joseon royal court sent a letter to Tsushima:

"The evidence clearly shows that Ulleung-do is ours... It's therefore a good thing that you've been stopping your people from fishing there."

The following reply came back:

"We will convey your country's opinion to the *bakufu*."

Thus it was that the controversy between Joseon and Japan over Ulleung-do and Dok-do came to an end. Thanks to An Yongbok's bold actions, Joseon secured firm evidence that the two islands were part of its territory, not that of Japan.

Far from a reward, however, harsh punishment awaited An back in Joseon. Leaving for another country without permission, together with impersonating a government official, were crimes that could have got him killed. Amid almost unanimous calls to have An executed, only two ministers, Nam Guman and Yun Jiwan, opposed such a sentence. Death was excessive, they said, since it was thanks to An that Japan had abandoned its claims to Ulleung-do and Dok-do and recognized the islands as Joseon territory. Sukjong endorsed their view and spared An's life, sending him into exile instead. What then became of him is unknown: we have no idea how long he survived, or what happened to his family.

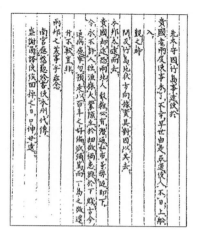

Japanese document
This document was written to inform Joseon, in January, 1697, that Japan recognized Ulleung-do Island as Joseon territory and would ban Japanese people from fishing there.
– National Archives of Japan

The Dok-do controversy resurfaces

It was during the presidency of Syngman Rhee in 1952, some 250 years after the deeds of An Yongbok, that the controversy over Dok-do reignited. Unlike the dispute 250 years earlier, this controversy revolved not around Ulleung-do but only Dok-do. As proof that the latter was part of its territory, Japan cited Shimane Prefectural Notice No. 40, a piece of legislation that reads:

"The uninhabited island located eighty-five nautical *ri* northwest of the Oki Islands at 37° 9' 30" north and 131° 55'

! Does Tsushima belong to Korea?

Tsushima is an island between the southeastern Korean Peninsula and Kyushu in Japan. In terms of distance, it's much closer to Korea than to Japan.

In the Joseon period, Tsushima played the role of a bridge for diplomacy and trade between Korea and Japan. All contact between the two states occurred via the island. After Park Wi conquered Tsushima in the late Goryeo period, Joseon politicians considered it part of their territory. Viewing Tsushima as the country's southern frontier, they entrusted diplomatic relations and trade with Japan to the island's feudal lord while supplying him with staple foods such as rice and soy beans.

These days, some claim Tsushima is also part of Korean territory. Just because we had it conquered at one point, however, doesn't mean it still belongs to us. Just as we can't now lay claim to Manchuria on the grounds that it used to be Goguryeo territory.

east is, henceforth, to be considered Japanese territory, called Takeshima and put under the jurisdiction of the governor of the Oki Islands in Shimane Prefecture, given the lack of admissible evidence that any other country is occupying it."

When this prefectural notice was issued in 1905, however, Korea remained completely in the dark. It only found out a year later, by which time it had lost its diplomatic rights to Japan as part of the Protectorate Treaty of 1905, was under Japanese control, and could no longer raise any objections.

What are Japan's grounds for claiming Dok-do? It asserts that the island was uninhabited and had no owner, that Japan knew about it before Joseon, that Japan's claim is legitimate since it made this unpopulated island its territory and informed the whole world about it, and that this claim is watertight in terms of international law, which currently recognizes the right to claim unowned territory.

In order, therefore to demolish Japan's claim, it's necessary to prove that Dok-do was not an uninhabited island but part of Korean territory. All Korea need do is present evidence, admissible according to international law, that Dok-do was already its territory in 1905, when Shimane Prefectural Notice No. 40 was issued.

Claims that Dok-do has been Korean territory since way

Dokdo (above) and lighthouse
The Dok-do issue is not just a territorial dispute. Economic and political factors are also part of the equation. The sea around Dok-do is a treasure trove of fish and other seafood, further motivating each side to claim ownership.

Japanese map showing Dok-do

This map appears in *Sangoku tsuran zusetsu* ("An Illustrated Description of Three Countries"), a 1785 book by Japanese scholar Hayashi Shihei. Ulleung-do and Dok-do are marked as Joseon territory.

–Seoul Museum of History

back in the Silla period, or that it's indicated as part of Korea on old maps, or that it's geographically closer to Korea than to Japan, or that it counts, in geological terms, as part of Korea's Baekdu Range, don't carry much weight in the eyes of international law. After all, there are lots of old maps and records claiming it as Japanese territory, too.

Unfortunately, Korea has not yet succeeded in producing anything that can be recognized as valid evidence according to international law. The Dok-do controversy has dragged on for more than sixty years already. During this time, it has repeatedly surfaced as something of a fashionable dispute for a while before dying back down again. Korean politicians and historians have apparently neglected to study the issue with the thoroughness and persistence required. In Japan, meanwhile, the general public, with the exception of a handful politicians and others, is largely uninterested in Dok-do. Those few interested people, however, have been remarkable in the detail of their research.

If Koreans want Dok-do to be recognized by the international community as their territory, they need to research the issue more calmly and tenaciously, until they can produce incontrovertible evidence.

Hendrik Hamel and Park Yeon:
Joseon's two Dutchmen

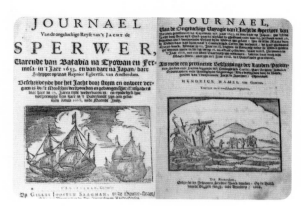

On the stormy night of August 15, 1653, a ship was wrecked off the coast of Jeju-do. The sun rose the next morning to reveal several exhausted sailors who had collapsed on the beach after managing to pull themselves out of the raging sea. There were thirty-six of them altogether.

Cover of 'Journael'
Hamel, a ship's clerk, knew how to make and record thorough observations. His book, *Journael*, was translated into French, German and English, becoming an international bestseller. The version on the left was published in Amsterdam in 1668, and that on the right in Rotterdam in the same year.

The men were merchants who had been on their way to Japan from the Netherlands, having already stopped in Indonesia and Taiwan. One of them was named Hendrik Hamel.

A few days later, Hamel and the other Dutchmen met the local governor, Yi wonjin, who gave them a house in which to stay. This was the same house that Gwanghaegun had dwelt in while in exile on Jeju-do.

Two months after the shipwreck, Hamel and his party found themselves face to face with a tall man with a yellow beard reaching all the way down to his chest.

"My name is Jan Janse de Weltevree," he said. "I come from De Rijp. I was shipwrecked on my way from Holland to Japan, and washed up here."

Hamel and the others were amazed and delighted just to meet a fellow countrymen in this strange land. Weltevree, however, was no longer Dutch. He had arrived in Joseon twenty-six years earlier, in 1628, the year after the first Manchu invasion. Since then, he had acquired Joseon nationality, taken the name Park Yeon, married a Joseon woman and had two children, a boy and a girl. Park had joined the Hullyeondogam, a training unit of the Joseon army, and fought in the war against the Manchus.

With Park acting as their interpreter, Hamel's party met King Hyojong and pleaded with him:

"We lost our ship in a storm and ended up drifting to Korea. If you send us to Japan, we'll get help from Dutch people there, return to our country and be reunited with our families and friends."

Hyojong refused their request:

"Joseon is not in the habit of sending back foreigners that enter the country. You must resign yourselves to spending the rest of your lives here. We'll give you everything you need to live."

The king threw a banquet for the men and gave them two sets of *hanbok* each. He then ordered them to work with Park Yeon in the Hullyeondogam, engaging in regular firing practice and fulfilling duties such as guarding royal processions. Park, meanwhile, was charged with teaching the men about the customs and culture of Joseon.

By now, Hamel and the other Dutchmen had become the talk of the town. They were invited to dinner at *yangban* homes, where they were made to sing songs and demonstrate their shooting prowess. Children were their biggest fans, thanks to a rumor that they drank by tilting their heads back and pouring liquid in through their noses.

Two years later, after several of the Dutchmen created trouble in Hanyang,

Memorial to Hamel
On the coast at Seogwipo, at the spot where Hamel and his fellow Dutchmen first stepped foot on Jeju-do, stands this memorial. It was built in 1980 after the Dutch and Korean governments each contributed 10,000 dollars.

they were banished to Jeolla-do Province. Life in exile was hard, but time kept passing and soon they had been there for ten years. Hamel and eight of his fellow seamen now succeeded in acquiring a boat and escaping from Joseon. From there, they went first to Japan, then back to Holland.

Hamel had lived in Joseon for thirteen years and twenty-eight days. He now wrote down everything he had seen, heard and experienced there in the form of a book titled *Journael*. His life in Korea was one of ups and downs, bringing him into contact with everyone from the king and top officials in the capital to poor commoners in the countryside. *Journael* therefore contains vivid descriptions of the lives of various people in seventeenth-century Joseon. It was first published in Amsterdam in 1668.

Park Yeon remained in Joseon until his death. The son he bore with a Joseon woman became a soldier.

Museum

Picture

Map

———

Historical records and books

《고려사(高麗史)》

《태조실록(太祖實錄)》

《태종실록(太宗實錄)》

《세종실록(世宗實錄)》

《연산군일기(燕山君日記)》

《중종실록(中宗實錄)》

《명종실록(明宗實錄)》

《선조실록(宣祖實錄)》

《인조실록(仁祖實錄)》

《숙종실록(肅宗實錄)》

홍량호(洪良浩), 강병도 역,《해동명장전(海東名將傳)》, 한국문화사, 1996

유희춘(柳希春), 이백순 역,《미암일기(眉巖日記)》 1-5, 담양군, 2004

이문건(李文楗),《묵재일기(默齋日記)》상.하, 한국사료총서 41, 국사편찬위원회, 1998

이문건(李文楗), 이상주 역주,《양아록(養兒錄)》, 태학사, 1997

조식(曺植), 경상대 남명학연구소 편역,《남명집(南冥集)》, 이론과실천, 1995

한우근 외 역,《역주 경국대전(經國大典) 번역편》《역주 경국대전 주석편》, 한국정신문화연구원, 1985-1986

기대승(奇大升),《고봉집(高峰集)》

《기묘록속집(己卯錄續集)》

《국조보감(國朝寶鑑)》

이긍익(李肯翊),《연려실기술(練藜室記述)》

성삼문(成三問), 최영성 옮김,《역주 매죽헌(梅竹軒) 문집》, 심산문화, 2002

성현(成俔),《용재총화(慵齋叢話)》

이이(李珥),《석담일기(石潭日記)》

이덕무(李德懋),《청장관전서(靑莊館全書)》

이유태(李惟泰),《정훈(庭訓)》

서울대학교 천연물과학연구소 편,《고사촬요(故事撮要)》.증보 산
림경제.고사신서》, 오름, 1994

이익(李瀷),《성호사설(星湖僿說)》

곽재우(郭再祐), 이재호 역주,《국역 망우선생문집》, 집문당, 2002

이순신(李舜臣), 허경진 옮김,《난중일기(亂中日記)》, 한양출판, 1997

남평 조씨, 전형대.박경신 역주,《병자일기(丙子日記)》, 예전사, 1991

작자 미상, 김광순 옮김,《산성일기(山城日記)》, 서해문집, 2004

소현세자(昭顯世子) 시강원(侍講院), 정하영 외 역,《심양장계(瀋陽狀啓)》, 창비, 2008

이건창(李建昌), 이덕일.이준녕 해역,《당의통략(黨議通略)》, 자유문고, 1998

안용복(安龍福)장군기념사업회,《안용복 장군-울릉도.독도의 내력》, 1967

김의환 엮음, 이태길 옮김,《증보 안용복 장군 - 붙임; 울릉도 독도의 역사》, 지평, 1996

William Eliot Griffis, Hendrik Hamel's Narrative of Captivity and Travels in Corea, Annotated, *COREA, WITHOUT AND WITHIN*, Presbyterian Board of Publication, Philadelphia, 1885, 이병도 역주,《하멜 표류기 - 부(附) 조선국기(朝鮮國記)》, 일조각, 1995

조선왕조실록(朝鮮王朝實錄)   http://sillok.history.go.kr

한국고전번역원   http://www.minchu.or.kr

한영우,《정도전 사상의 연구》, 서울대학교출판부, 1983

John B. Duncan, *Origins of the Chŏson Dynasty*, University of Washington Press, Seattle, WA, USA, 2000, 김범 옮김,《조선 왕조의 기원》, 너머북스, 2013

홍순민,《우리 궁궐 이야기》, 청년사, 1999

임덕순,《600년 수도 서울》, 지식산업사, 1994

강신항,《훈민정음 연구》, 성균관대출판부, 1999

김민수,《신(新) 국어학사》, 일조각, 1985

최경봉.시정곤.박영준,《한글에 대해 알아야 할 모든 것》, 책과함께, 2008

권태욱 외,《한국중세사회의 음악문화; 조선 전기편》, 한국예술종합학교 전통예술원, 2002

정홍준,《조선 중기 정치권력구조 연구》, 고려대학교 민족문화연구소, 1996

조좌호,《한국과거제도사연구》, 범우사, 1996

미야지마 히로시(宮島博史), 노영구 옮김,《양반》, 강, 1996

황영선,《황희의 생애와 사상》, 국학자료원, 1998

신명호,《조선의 왕》, 가람기획, 1998

이복규,《묵재일기에 나타난 조선전기의 민속》, 민속원, 1999

이종호,《화담 서경덕》, 일지사, 1998

유정동 편저,《퇴계의 생애와 사상》, 박영사, 1974

이수건,《영남사림파의 형성》, 영남대학교출판부, 1979

한국사상사연구회 편저,《조선 유학의 학파들》, 예문서원, 1996

정우영.이정일.정상훈,《역주 속 삼강행실도》, 한국문화사, 2008

김기춘 편저,《조선시대 형전 －경국대전 형전을 중심으로》, 삼영사, 1990

김영두 옮김,《퇴계와 고봉, 편지를 쓰다》, 소나무, 2003

김돈,《조선전기 군신권력관계 연구》, 서울대학교출판부, 1997

김범,《사화와 반정의 시대》, 역사비평사, 2007

박덕규,《신숙주 평전》, 둥지, 1995

조효순,《복식》, 대원사, 1989

신영훈,《한국의 살림집》, 열화당, 1983

심우성,《우리나라 민속놀이》, 동문선, 1996

신양선,《조선후기 서지사 연구》, 혜안, 1996

김두종,《한국고인쇄기술사》, 탐구당, 1995

정형우,《조선조 서적문화연구》, 구미무역주식회사출판부, 1995

정석종,《조선후기사회변동연구》, 일조각, 1983

홍명희,《임꺽정》 1-10, 사계절, 1985

황석영,《장길산》 1-10, 현암사, 1983-1984

허경진,《홍길동전》, 책세상, 2004

허경진,《허균 평전》, 돌베개, 2002

이윤석,《홍길동전 연구-서지와 해석》, 계명대출판부, 1997

설성경,《홍길동전의 비밀》, 서울대학교출판부, 2004

이장희,《임진왜란사 연구》, 아세아문화사, 1999

한명기,《임진왜란과 한중관계》, 역사비평사, 1999

한명기,《광해군》, 역사비평사, 2000

곽차섭,《조선 청년 안토니오 코레아, 루벤스를 만나다》, 푸른역사, 2004

김재근,《거북선》, 정우사, 1992

남천우,《유물의 재발견》, 학고재, 1997

이희환,《조선후기 당쟁연구》, 국학자료원, 1995

이은순,《조선후기 당쟁사연구》, 일지사, 1988

이성무.정만조 외,《조선후기 당쟁의 종합적 검토》, 한국정신문화연구원, 1992

박성순,《선비의 배반》, 고즈원, 2004

이영춘,《조선후기 왕위계승 연구》, 집문당, 1998

이진명,《독도, 지리상의 재발견》, 삼인, 1998

신용하,《독도의 민족영토사 연구》, 지식산업사, 1996

한일관계사연구회,《독도와 대마도》, 지성의샘, 1996

손승철,《조선시대 한일관계사연구》, 지성의샘, 1996

정구복.박광용.이영훈.최진옥.박연호,《조선시대 연구사》, 한국정신문화연구원, 1999

국사편찬위원회,《한국사》 26-31, 1995-1998

강만길 외,《한국사》 7-8, 한길사, 1995

한국역사연구회,《조선시대 사람들은 어떻게 살았을까》 1-2, 청년사, 1996

한국고문서학회 엮음,《조선시대 생활사》, 역사비평사, 1996

박한용.장원정.황경,《시와 이야기가 있는 우리역사》 1, 동녘, 1996

젊은역사연구모임,《영화처럼 읽는 한국사》, 명진출판, 1999

이이화,《한국사 이야기 9; 조선의 건국》, 한길사, 2000

전국역사교사모임,《살아있는 한국사 교과서》 1, 휴머니스트, 2002

한국생활사박물관 편찬위원회,《한국생활사박물관》 9-11, 2003-2004

이야기 한국역사 편집위원회,《이야기 한국역사》 6-8, 풀빛,

1997

이기백,《신수판(新修版) 한국사신론》, 일조각, 1994

변태섭,《한국사 통론(通論)》, 삼영사, 1986

한국역사연구회,《한국역사》, 역사비평사, 1992

한국사특강편찬위원회 편,《한국사 특강》, 서울대학교 출판부, 1990

한국역사연구회,《한국사강의》, 한울아카데미, 1989

역사문제연구소,《사진과 그림으로 보는 한국의 역사》2, 웅진닷컴, 1993

구로 역사연구소,《바로 보는 우리 역사》1, 거름, 1990

한국민중사연구회 편,《한국민중사》1, 풀빛, 1986

박은봉,《한국사 상식 바로잡기》, 책과함께, 2007

박은봉,《한권으로 보는 한국사 100장면》, 가람기획, 1993 /《개정판 한국사 100장면》, 실천문학사, 1997

박은봉,《한국사 뒷이야기》, 실천문학사, 1997

박은봉,《세계사 뒷이야기》, 실천문학사, 1994

박은봉,《엄마의 역사편지》2, 웅진주니어, 2000

Academic papers and essays

이형우, 고려 우왕대의 정치적 추이와 정치세력 연구, 고려대학교 박사논문, 1999

이형우, 정몽주의 정치활동에 대한 일고찰-공양왕 대를 중심으로,《사학연구》41, 1990

김당택, 고려 우왕대 이성계와 정몽주.정도전의 정치적 결합,《역사학보》158, 1998

유창규, 고려말 최영 세력의 형성과 요동공략,《역사학보》143, 1994

허흥식, 고려말 이성계(1335-1408)의 세력기반,《고병익선생회갑기념 사학논총》, 1984

홍순민, 궁궐플레이-왕은 왜 궁궐을 옮겨다녔을까,《역사비평》, 1996 겨울호

홍순민, 조선 왕조 궁궐 경영과 양궐체제의 변천, 서울대 박사논문, 1996

젊은역사연구모임, 백성의 글, 훈민정음의 창제,《영화처럼 읽는 한국사》, 명진출판, 1999

이기문, 훈민정음 친제론,《한국문화》13, 1992

이기문, 훈민정음의 창제,《한국사》26, 국사편찬위원회, 1995

김민수, 훈민정음 창제와 최항,《새국어생활》14, 2004

김남이, 집현전 학사의 문학 연구, 이화여대 박사논문, 2001

최승희, 집현전 연구,《역사학보》32-33, 1966-1967

정연식, 아! 고달픈 신참생활,《일상으로 본 조선시대 이야기》1, 청년사, 2001

이장희, 청백리제도의 사적 고찰,《수둔 박영석교수 회갑기념 한국사학논총》상, 1992

이서행, 조선조 청백리의 공직윤리에 관한 연구, 단국대학교 박사논문, 1987

심희기, 16세기 이문건가의 노비에 대한 체벌의 실태분석,《국사관논총》97, 2001

문철영, 고려말.조선초 백정의 신분과 차역,《한국사론》26, 1991

유승원, 조선 초기의 '신량역천' 계층,《한국사론》1, 1973

박은봉, 2월의 인물-실천철학을 강조한 남명 조식,《지방행정》, 지방행정공제회, 1995

김충렬, 생애를 통해서 본 남명의 위인,《대동문화연구》17, 1983

김범, 조선전기 '훈구.사림세력' 연구의 재검토,《한국사학보》15, 2003

Edward W. Wagner, *Literati Purges: Political Conflict in Early Yi KOREA*, Cambridge, Mass: East Asian Research Center, Harvard University Press, 1974, 송준호 역, 정치사적 입장에서 본 조선 사화의 성격,《역사학보》85, 1980 / 이훈상.손숙경 옮김,《조선왕조 사회의 성취와 귀속》, 일조각, 2007

송수환, 갑자사화의 새 해석,《사학연구》57, 1999

박한용.장원정.황경, 금삼의 파,《시와 이야기가 있는 우리역사》1, 동녘, 1996

박한용.장원정.황경, 조광조와 도덕 정치,《시와 이야기가 있는 우리역사》1, 동녘, 1996

이태진, 사림과 서원,《한국사》12, 국사편찬위원회, 1978 /《조선유교사회사론》, 지식산업사, 1989 재수록

안병희, 신숙주의 생애와 학문, 《10월의 문화인물》, 국립국어연구원, 2002

강문식, 집현전 출신 관인(官人)의 학문관과 정치관, 서울대 박사논문, 1997

한복진, 의식주 생활, 《한국사》 34, 국사편찬위원회, 1995

김정미, 조선시대 사람들의 패션 감각, 《조선시대 사람들은 어떻게 살았을까》 2, 청년사, 1996

정연식, 조선시대의 끼니, 《한국사연구》 112, 2001

정연식, 새벽에도 먹은 점심, 《일상으로 본 조선시대 이야기》 2, 청년사, 2001

정연식, 조선시대의 식생활과 음식문화, 《조선시대 사람들은 어떻게 살았을까》 1, 청년사, 1996

우인수, 조선후기 한 사족가의 생활양식-초려(草廬) 이유태의 정훈(庭訓)을 중심으로, 《조선시대사학보》 12, 2000.3.

박정규, 조선왕조시대의 전근대적 신문에 관한 연구, 서울대 박사논문, 1982

김경수, '조보'의 발행과 그 성격, 《사학연구》 58.59, 1999

차배근, 우리나라 조보에 대한 신문학적 분석 고, 《서울대 신문연구소 학보》 17, 1980

김영주, 조보에 대한 몇가지 쟁점, 《한국언론정보학보》, 2008 가을(통권 43호)

이혜은, 조선조 문헌의 발행부수와 보급에 관한 연구, 숙명여대 석사논문, 1996

김치우, 《고사활요》의 서지적 연구, 성균관대학교 석사논문, 1972

矢澤康祐, 임거정(林巨正)의 반란과 그 사회적 배경, 《전통시대의 민중운동》 상, 풀빛, 1981

임형택, 역사 속의 홍길동과 소설 속의 홍길동, 《역사비평》 17, 1992 여름호

이능우, 홍길동전과 허균의 관계, 《국어국문학》 42.43, 1969

장효현, 홍길동전의 생성과 유전(流傳)에 대하여, 《국어국문학》 129, 2001

김광순, 홍길동전의 작가시비에 대하여, 《문화전통논집》 창간호, 부산경성대 향토문화연구소, 1993

김진세, 홍길동전의 작자 고(攷)-하나의 가설제기를 위하여, 《서울대논문집》 1, 1969

이진희, 임란 경복궁 방화주범은 왜군, 〈부산국제신보〉 1991년 6월 15일자, 《정내암사상연구논총》 제1집, 내암선생기념사업회, 1995

박한용.장원정.황경, 관산의 달을 보며 통곡하노라, 《시와 이야기가 있는 우리역사》 1, 동녘, 1996

정성일, 조선 도공의 후예, 또칠이와 이삼평, 《한국과 일본, 왜곡과 콤플렉스의 역사》 1, 자작나무, 1998

김현덕, 한국 천주교 전래의 기원설에 대한 비판연구-1566년부터 1784년까지, 가톨릭대학교 대학원 석사논문, 1993

최영희, 귀선고(龜船考), 《사총》 제3집, 1958

김용흠, 병자호란기의 주화(主和).척화(斥和) 논쟁, 《동방학지》 135, 2006

이이화, 최명길; 실리와 타협의 정치가, 《이야기 인물한국사》 3, 한길사, 1993

김용덕, 소현세자연구, 《조선후기사상사연구》, 을유문화사, 1977

홍순민, 장희빈을 위한 변명, 《역사비평》 1991 가을호

Joseon - From founding to later years

Letters from Korean History

Volume III

First Published 5 May 2016
Third Published 10 April 2023

Author | Park Eunbong
Translator | Ben Jackson
Illustrator | Illustration: Lee Sanggwon, Map: Yu Sanghyeon

Design | Lee Seokwoon, Kim Miyeon

Published by | Cum Libro Inc. **CUM LIBRO** 책과함께
Address | 2F, Sowaso Bldg. 70, Donggyo-ro, Mapo-gu, Seoul, Korea 04022
Tel | (+82) 2-335-1982
Fax | (+82) 2-335-1316
E-mail | prpub@daum.net
Blog | blog.naver.com/prpub
Registered | 3 April 2003 No. 25100-2003-392

ISBN 979-11-86293-50-8 04740
ISBN 979-11-86293-46-1 (set)